Betty Crocker's

RED SPOON COLLECTION™

BEST RECIPES FOR
MEAT AND VEGETABLES

PRENTICE
HALL
PRESS

New York   London   Toronto   Sydney   Tokyo   Singapore

PRENTICE HALL PRESS
15 Columbus Circle
New York, New York 10023

Published simultaneously in Canada by Prentice Hall Canada Inc.

PRENTICE HALL PRESS and colophons are registered
trademarks of Simon & Schuster, Inc.

BETTY CROCKER is a registered trademark
of General Mills, Inc.

RED SPOON COLLECTION is a trademark of General Mills, Inc.

Library of Congress Cataloging-in-Publication Data

Best recipes for meat and vegetables.
    p.   cm.—(Betty Crocker's red spoon collection)
    Includes index.
    ISBN 0-13-068362-0
    1. Cookery (Meat) 2. Cookery (Vegetables) I. Series.
TX749.B4143 1991
641.6'6—dc20
                                            90-39879
                                            CIP

Manufactured in the United States of America

10 9 8 7 6 5 4 3 2 1

First Edition

**Front Cover: Grilled Italian Sausage
Kabobs (page 93)**

CONTENTS

INTRODUCTION

Meat and vegetables are the mainstay of our American cuisine, helping us to get a proper balance of protein, vitamins and fiber. The two complement each other—what would liver be without onions, or Yankee Pot Roast without succulently cooked potatoes, carrots, onions and other tender treasures nestled in its richly blended juices?

The term *a meat and potatoes man* has become part of our language, meaning someone who likes the basics without excessive frills. Since a potato is a vegetable, a man or a woman who wants "meat and potatoes" is actually asking for a well-balanced, tasty meal. A perfectly cooked steak and steaming baked potato paired with a crisp green salad is a meal that would make the end of almost any day perfect. But you can't have the same meal every day, and coming up with suggestions beyond steak and potatoes that still incorporate their taste, ease and nutrition is the purpose of this book.

Break Away from the Bland

Anything viewed without creativity and imagination is in danger of becoming bland and ho-hum. When planning meals, it helps to jog your brain with new ideas so that old favorites don't become yesterday's news. Pot roast makes a good Sunday dinner, but Mexican Pot Roast (page 12) or Pork Tenderloin in Tequila (page 20) makes Sunday dinner an event. The section on roasts included here will help give your menus added interest and variety.

While roasts are wonderful on days when you have time to cook your meat and vegetables slowly and enjoy the subtle flavors of a long-cooking dish, some nights you need a meal that you can cook quickly on top of the stove. A quick and tasty stove-top meal is also full of flavor and good nutrition. Spice up your old standbys with new skillet dishes—Spicy Stir-fried Beef (page 21), Ham and Zucchini with Poppy Seed (page 32) and Pork Chops in Radish Sauce (page 32) are just a few of the hurry-up recipes you can make in a skillet.

Meat and vegetables lend themselves perfectly to soups and stews. A hearty stew bubbling on the stove can warm a cold winter day, and its stick-to-the-ribs ability satisfies the heartiest appetite. Choose a spicy soup such as Southwest Black Bean Soup (page 60), or a reinvented classic such as Beef Stew with Chutney (pages 66–67) or an old favorite such as Hungarian Beef

Goulash (page 64) and serve with crusty bread and butter for a satisfying meal.

The combinations of meat and vegetables are almost endless, and their variety is temptingly displayed in the chapter Different Dinners. Try Spinach Manicotti (page 82), Pork Florentine (page 88) or Pork and Broccoli Risotto (page 92) for exotic flavor; Beef and Corn Pie (page 86) and Stuffed Rolled Steak (page 78) to fill a traditional yen.

And of course casseroles are well represented, their ease and versatility a natural for meat and vegetables. Whether you make Beef Burgundy (page 39), African Beef and Rice (page 39) or Meatballs with Mixed Vegetables (page 45), make two casseroles at a time and freeze one for later use; you'll be ahead of the game on a night when you are tired and hungry.

Terrific Tips

In the back of this book are Red Spoon Tips that will tell you how to select, tenderize, roast and microwave various cuts of meat, as well as how to select the freshest and most delicious vegetables. With these tips and the recipes collected here, you will find that meat and vegetables can be much more than just basic nutrition. They can be delicious and inventive meals that satisfy your imagination as well as your need for "meat and potatoes."

· 1 ·

ROASTS

French Beef Roast

6 SERVINGS

3-pound beef boneless chuck or rolled
   rump roast
1 teaspoon salt
1 teaspoon dried thyme leaves
1 bay leaf
1 large clove garlic, cut into fourths
6 whole cloves
5 peppercorns
4 cups water
4 medium carrots, cut crosswise into
   halves
2 medium onions, cut into fourths
2 medium turnips, cut into fourths
2 medium stalks celery, cut into 1-inch
   pieces

Place beef, salt, thyme, bay leaf, garlic, cloves and peppercorns in 4-quart Dutch oven; add water. Heat to boiling; reduce heat. Cover and simmer 2½ hours. Add remaining ingredients. Cover and simmer until beef and vegetables are tender, about 30 minutes. Remove beef; cut into ¼-inch slices. Serve vegetables with beef. Strain broth; serve with beef and vegetables.

PRESSURE COOKER DIRECTIONS: Decrease water to 2 cups. Place beef, salt, thyme, bay leaf, garlic, cloves and peppercorns in 6-quart pressure cooker; add water. Following manufacturer's directions, cover and cook at 15 pounds pressure 1 hour. Cool 5 minutes; reduce pressure. Add remaining ingredients. Cover and cook at 15 pounds pressure 8 minutes. Cool 5 minutes; reduce pressure. Remove beef; cut into ¼-inch slices. Serve vegetables with beef. Strain broth; serve with beef and vegetables.

French Boiled Dinner

1½-pound beef boneless chuck roast
1 marrow bone, if desired
8 black peppercorns
1 teaspoon salt
¼ teaspoon dried thyme leaves
1 bay leaf
4 cups water
1½ pounds chicken drumsticks
10 to 12 small carrots
10 to 12 small onions or 3 large onions,
    cut into fourths
3 medium turnips, cut into fourths
4 stalks celery, cut into 1-inch pieces
¾ teaspoon salt
⅛ teaspoon pepper

Place beef, marrow bone, peppercorns, 1 teaspoon salt, thyme and bay leaf in Dutch oven. Add water. Heat to boiling; reduce heat. Cover and simmer 1 hour. Add chicken; cover and simmer 1 hour longer.

Add carrots, onions, turnips and celery; sprinkle with ¾ teaspoon salt and pepper. Cover and simmer until beef and vegetables are tender, about 45 minutes. Remove chicken and vegetables to warm platter; slice beef. Strain broth; serve in soup bowls.

Dutch Boiled Dinner

2-pound beef brisket
1½ cups water
1 teaspoon salt
4 medium potatoes, pared and cut into
    fourths
4 medium carrots, sliced
3 medium onions, chopped (about
    1½ cups)
1½ teaspoons salt
¼ teaspoon pepper
Snipped parsley
Prepared mustard or horseradish

Heat beef, water and 1 teaspoon salt to boiling in Dutch oven; reduce heat. Cover and simmer 1½ hours. Add potatoes, carrots and onions; sprinkle with 1½ teaspoons salt and the pepper. Cover and simmer until beef and vegetables are tender, about 45 minutes.

Drain meat and vegetables, reserving broth. Mash vegetables or puree in food mill; mound on heated platter. Cut beef across grain into thin slices; arrange around vegetables. Garnish with parsley; serve with reserved broth and the mustard.

New England Pot Roast

*4-pound beef arm, blade or cross rib pot
 roast**
1½ teaspoons salt
1 teaspoon pepper
*½ jar (8 ounce size) prepared
 horseradish, if desired*
1 cup water
8 small potatoes, cut into halves
8 medium carrots, cut into fourths
8 small onions
Kettle Gravy (below)

Cook beef in 12-inch skillet or Dutch oven over medium heat until brown; reduce heat. Sprinkle with salt and pepper. Spread horseradish over both sides of beef. Add water. Heat to boiling; reduce heat. Cover and simmer on top of range or cook in 325° oven 2½ hours.

Add potatoes, carrots and onions. Cover and cook until beef and vegetables are tender, about 1 hour. Place beef and vegetables on warm platter; keep warm while preparing Kettle Gravy.

*3-pound beef bottom round, rolled rump, tip or chuck eye roast can be substituted. Increase salt to 2 teaspoons.

KETTLE GRAVY

Beef broth from New England Pot Roast
Water
½ cup cold water
¼ cup all-purpose flour

Skim excess fat from beef broth. Add enough water to broth to measure 2 cups. Shake ½ cup cold water and flour in tightly covered container. (For a smooth mixture, it is important to add the flour to the water.) Stir flour mixture gradually into drippings. Heat to boiling, stirring constantly. Boil and stir 1 minute.

Following pages: New England Pot Roast

Mexican Pot Roast

6-pound beef arm, blade or cross rib pot
  roast
8 cloves garlic
4 slices bacon, cut into halves
2 teaspoons salt
1/2 teaspoon pepper
1/2 cup prepared mustard
1/4 cup vegetable oil
1/2 cup chopped carrot
1/2 cup chopped celery
1/2 cup sliced mushrooms
2 tablespoons snipped fresh cilantro
1 teaspoon ground nutmeg
1 teaspoon ground thyme
2 jalapeño chilies, seeded and finely
  chopped
2 bay leaves
1 medium onion, chopped (about 1/2 cup)
1 bottle or can (12 ounces) beer

Make a 1½-inch-deep cut across beef roast. Wrap each clove garlic in 1 piece bacon; insert in cut. Sprinkle beef with salt and pepper; spread with mustard. Cover and refrigerate at least 4 hours.

Cook beef in oil in 4-quart Dutch oven over medium heat until brown. Stir in remaining ingredients. Heat to boiling; reduce heat. Cover and simmer until beef is tender, about 2½ hours.

Remove beef to warm platter. Remove bay leaves from broth. Skim fat from broth. Place 2 cups of the broth and vegetables in blender container; cover and blend on medium speed until smooth. Serve with beef.

Oriental Pot Roast

4-pound beef arm, blade or cross rib pot roast
1 can (15¼ ounces) pineapple chunks in juice
1 large onion, sliced
3 tablespoons soy sauce
1 teaspoon ground ginger
1 large clove garlic, crushed
2 medium stalks celery, diagonally sliced (about 1 cup)
1 package (10 ounces) frozen spinach leaves, thawed
1 can (4 ounces) mushroom stems and pieces, drained

Cook beef in 4-quart Dutch oven over medium heat until brown. Drain pineapple; reserve juice. Place onion on beef. Mix pineapple juice, soy sauce, ginger and garlic; pour over beef. Heat to boiling; reduce heat. Cover and simmer until tender, about 2½ hours. Add celery. Cover and simmer 20 minutes. Add pineapple chunks, spinach and mushrooms. Cover and simmer 5 minutes. Remove beef, pineapple and vegetables. Skim fat from broth; serve broth with beef.

PRESSURE COOKER DIRECTIONS: Cook beef in 6-quart pressure cooker over medium heat until brown. Drain pineapple; reserve juice. Place onion on beef. Mix pineapple juice, soy sauce, ginger and garlic; pour over beef. Following manufacturer's directions, cover and cook at 15 pounds pressure 35 to 45 minutes. Cool 5 minutes; reduce pressure. Add celery. Cover and cook at 15 pounds pressure 5 minutes. Cool 5 minutes; reduce pressure. Add pineapple chunks, spinach and mushrooms. Uncover and cook until pineapple chunks are hot, about 5 minutes. Remove beef, pineapple and vegetables. Skim fat from broth; serve broth with beef.

Company Pot Roast

3- to 4-pound beef rolled rump roast*
3 tablespoons vegetable oil
¾ cup dairy sour cream
¾ cup dry red wine
½ teaspoon salt
½ teaspoon pepper
½ teaspoon dried thyme leaves
2 cloves garlic, finely chopped
2 medium carrots, cut crosswise into
  1-inch pieces
2 medium onions, sliced and separated
  into rings
½ cup water
2 tablespoons all-purpose flour
1 tablespoon lemon juice

Cook beef roast in oil in 4-quart ovenproof Dutch oven until brown; remove beef. Mix remaining ingredients except water, flour and lemon juice in Dutch oven.

Return beef to Dutch oven. Cover and bake in 325° oven until beef is tender, about 3½ hours. Remove beef to heated platter; keep warm while preparing gravy.

Skim fat from liquid. Shake water and flour in tightly covered container; gradually stir into liquid. Heat to boiling, stirring constantly. Boil and stir 1 minute. Stir in lemon juice; cook 1 minute. Slice beef thinly; serve with gravy.

*Beef bottom round or boneless chuck eye roast can be substituted for the rolled rump roast.

TO MICROWAVE: Omit oil; increase flour to 3 tablespoons. Place 3-pound beef roast in 3-quart microwavable casserole. Cover tightly and microwave on high 12 minutes; drain.

Mix remaining ingredients except water, flour and lemon juice; add to casserole, spooning some of mixture over beef. Cover tightly and microwave 10 minutes; rotate casserole ½ turn. Microwave on medium-low (30%) 1 hour; turn beef over. Cover tightly and microwave until beef is tender, 45 minutes to 1 hour longer. Remove beef and vegetables to heated platter; keep warm.

Mix water and flour and stir into liquid as directed above. Microwave uncovered on high 2 minutes; stir in lemon juice. Microwave uncovered until thickened, 1 to 2 minutes longer. Serve beef as directed above.

Yankee Pot Roast

1/4 cup all-purpose flour
2 teaspoons salt
1/2 teaspoon pepper
4- to 5-pound beef boneless shoulder pot
    roast
1 tablespoon shortening
1/2 cup water
2 cups sliced celery
3 medium potatoes, pared and cut into
    1/2-inch cubes (about 2 cups)
2 cups diced carrots
2 cups 1/2-inch cubes rutabaga or yellow
    turnips
1 cup chopped onion

Mix flour, salt and pepper; rub over beef roast. Heat shortening in skillet or Dutch oven until melted; brown beef on all sides. Drain off fat; add water. Heat to boiling; reduce heat. Cover tightly and simmer on top of range or in 325° oven 2 hours.

Add vegetables. Add 1/4 cup water if necessary. Cover and simmer until beef and vegetables are tender, 45 to 60 minutes.

Pot Roast, Western Style

1 cup water
1 cup pitted prunes (about 1/2 pound)*
2 teaspoons salt
1/2 teaspoon ground ginger
1/4 teaspoon pepper
4- to 5-pound beef boneless shoulder pot
    roast
1 tablespoon shortening
3 medium onions, chopped (about
    1 1/2 cups)
2 cloves garlic, finely chopped
1/2 cup water or dry red wine
1 can (6 ounces) pitted ripe olives,
    drained
5 ounces mushrooms, sliced (about 2 cups)

Pour 1 cup water over prunes; reserve. Mix salt, ginger and pepper; rub over beef roast. Heat shortening in skillet or Dutch oven until melted; brown beef on all sides. Drain off fat; add onions, garlic and 1/2 cup water. Heat to boiling; reduce heat. Cover tightly and simmer on top of range or in 325° oven 2 hours.

Add prunes, olives and mushrooms. Cover and cook until beef is tender, about 1 hour.

*1 cup dried apricots, cut into halves, can be substituted for the prunes.

Following pages: Pot Roast, Western Style

Roast Veal

5-pound veal shoulder (arm or blade) or
  rolled rump roast
1 clove garlic, halved
¼ cup all-purpose flour
¾ teaspoon salt
½ teaspoon dried savory leaves
½ teaspoon ground thyme
½ teaspoon sage
¼ teaspoon allspice
⅛ teaspoon pepper
⅓ cup shortening
4 carrots, sliced
2 celery stalks, diced
1 medium onion, minced
1 cup water
Gravy (below)

Rub surface of roast with garlic. Stir together flour, salt, savory, thyme, sage, allspice and pepper; rub mixture into roast. In open shallow roasting pan, brown meat in hot shortening over medium heat, about 15 minutes. Remove meat from pan. Add carrots, celery and onion; cook and stir just until onion is tender. Spread vegetables in pan; place meat on top and add water. Cover pan; place in 325° oven and braise about 2½ hours, until meat is tender. Remove meat and vegetables to hot platter; keep warm while preparing Gravy. Serve Gravy with meat and vegetables.

GRAVY

Drippings from Roast Veal
¼ cup all-purpose flour
Water

Pour drippings (meat juice and fat) into a bowl, leaving brown particles in pan. Let fat rise to top of drippings; skim off fat. Place ¼ cup fat in roasting pan; blend in flour. Cook over low heat, stirring until mixture is smooth and bubbly. Remove from heat. Measure meat juice; add water to measure 2 cups liquid and stir into flour mixture. Heat to boiling, stirring constantly. Boil and stir 1 minute. Makes 2 cups.

Roast Pork Loin with Sage Onions

4-pound pork boneless top loin roast
Salt
Pepper
2 pounds yellow onions
1¼ teaspoons ground sage
1 teaspoon salt
¼ teaspoon pepper
Gravy (below)

Place pork roast fat side up on rack in shallow roasting pan. Sprinkle with salt and pepper. Insert meat thermometer so tip is in center of thickest part of pork and does not rest in fat. Do not add water. Do not cover. Roast in 325° oven 1½ hours.

Heat 2 inches water to boiling. Add onions. Cover and heat to boiling. Cook until tender, 15 to 20 minutes; drain. Chop onions coarsely; stir in sage, 1 teaspoon salt and ¼ teaspoon pepper. Remove pork and rack from pan; pour off drippings, reserving ¼ cup for Gravy. Mound onion mixture in center of pan; place pork on top. Roast until meat thermometer registers 170°, about 1 hour.

GRAVY

¼ cup drippings, reserved from Roast
  Pork Loin with Sage Onions
¼ cup all-purpose flour
2 cups water
Salt
Pepper

Mix reserved drippings and flour. Cook over low heat, stirring constantly, until mixture is smooth and bubbly. Remove from heat; stir in water. Heat to boiling, stirring constantly. Boil and stir 1 minute. Season with salt and pepper.

PORK LOIN ROAST WITH SAUERKRAUT: Omit onions, sage, 1 teaspoon salt, ¼ teaspoon pepper and the Gravy. Mix 1 can (27 ounces) sauerkraut, drained, 1 medium onion, chopped (about ½ cup), ¼ cup water, 2 teaspoons sugar and 1 teaspoon instant beef bouillon. Mound in center of pan; place pork on top. Roast as directed.

Pork Tenderloin in Tequila

1/4 cup prepared mustard
2 pounds pork tenderloin
1/4 cup vegetable oil
2 cloves garlic, cut into halves
1/4 cup chopped carrot
1/4 cup chopped celery
1/4 cup lime juice
1/4 cup tequila
1 tablespoon ground red chilies
1 teaspoon salt
1 teaspoon dried oregano leaves
1 teaspoon dried thyme leaves
1/4 teaspoon pepper
4 medium tomatoes, chopped (about 4 cups)
1 small onion, chopped (about 1/4 cup)
1 bay leaf

Spread mustard over pork tenderloin. Heat oil and garlic in 10-inch skillet until hot. Cook pork in oil over medium heat until brown. Remove garlic.

Stir in remaining ingredients except parsley. Heat to boiling; reduce heat. Cover and simmer until pork is done, about 30 minutes. Remove bay leaf.

Pork with Cumin

2 pounds pork boneless shoulder, cut into
    1-inch cubes
1/4 cup all-purpose flour
1/2 cup vegetable oil
1 medium onion, chopped (about 1/2 cup)
2 slices bacon, cut up
1/2 cup water
2 tablespoons orange juice
2 tablespoons lime juice
2 teaspoons instant chicken bouillon
2 teaspoons cumin seed
1 teaspoon dried oregano leaves
1/2 teaspoon salt
1/4 teaspoon pepper
4 medium tomatoes, chopped (about 4 cups)
2 medium potatoes, diced
1/2 cup dairy sour cream

Coat pork with flour. Heat oil in 10-inch skillet until hot. Cook and stir pork in oil over medium heat until brown. Remove pork with slotted spoon; drain.

Cook and stir onion and bacon in same skillet until bacon is crisp. Stir in pork and remaining ingredients except sour cream. Heat to boiling; reduce heat. Cover and simmer until pork is done, about 45 minutes. Stir in sour cream; heat until hot.

· 2 ·

SKILLET DISHES

Spicy Stir-fried Beef

1½ pounds beef boneless sirloin steak
1 tablespoon cornstarch
1 tablespoon vegetable oil
1 tablespoon soy sauce
1 teaspoon sugar
¼ teaspoon salt
¼ teaspoon pepper
1 tablespoon soy sauce
¼ to ½ teaspoon finely crushed dried red
    pepper
2 tablespoons vegetable oil
1 teaspoon finely chopped gingerroot
2 large cloves garlic, finely chopped
1 large green pepper, cut into ¼-inch
    strips
2 medium carrots, shredded (about 1 cup)
1 can (8 ounces) bamboo shoots, drained
1 can (8 ounces) sliced water chestnuts
4 green onions (with tops), cut into 2-inch
    pieces

Trim fat from beef. Cut beef into 2-inch strips. Cut strip into ⅛-inch slices. Stack slices and cut into thin strips. (Beef is easier to slice if partially frozen.) Toss beef, cornstarch, 1 tablespoon oil, 1 tablespoon soy sauce, the sugar, salt and pepper in glass or plastic bowl. Cover and refrigerate 30 minutes. Mix 1 tablespoon soy sauce and the red pepper; let stand at room temperature.

Heat 2 tablespoons oil in 12-inch skillet or wok over high heat until hot. Add beef mixture, gingerroot and garlic; cook and stir until beef is brown, about 5 minutes. Add green pepper, carrots, bamboo shoots and water chestnuts; cook and stir 3 minutes. Add onions and red pepper mixture; cook and stir 1 minute.

Cantonese Beef

2 pounds beef boneless chuck, tip or
    round, cut into 1-inch cubes
1 small onion, chopped (about ¼ cup)
3 tablespoons shortening
1½ cups water
1 can (11 ounces) mandarin orange
    segments, drained (reserve syrup)
⅓ cup soy sauce
½ teaspoon ground ginger
2 tablespoons cornstarch
¼ cup cold water
1 small green pepper, cut into strips
8 ounces mushrooms, sliced
4 medium stalks celery, cut diagonally
    into ½-inch pieces
1 can (8 ounces) water chestnuts, drained
    and sliced

Cook and stir beef and onion in shortening in 10-inch skillet over medium heat until onion is tender; drain. Add 1½ cups water, the reserved orange syrup, soy sauce and ginger.

OVEN METHOD: Pour into ungreased 3-quart casserole or 13 × 9 × 2-inch baking dish. Cover and cook in 325° oven until beef is tender, 1¾ to 2 hours. Mix cornstarch and ¼ cup water; stir into beef mixture. Stir in green pepper, mushrooms, celery and water chestnuts. Cover and cook until celery is crisp-tender, 10 to 15 minutes. Fold in orange segments just before serving.

RANGE-TOP METHOD: Heat to boiling; reduce heat. Cover and simmer until beef is tender, about 1½ hours. Mix cornstarch and ¼ cup water; stir into beef mixture. Heat to boiling over medium heat, stirring constantly. Boil and stir 1 minute; reduce heat. Stir in green pepper, mushrooms, celery and water chestnuts. Cover and cook until celery is crisp-tender, 5 to 7 minutes. Fold in orange segments just before serving.

Sukiyaki

1 teaspoon instant beef bouillon
1/2 cup hot water
1/3 cup soy sauce
2 tablespoons sugar
1-pound beef tenderloin or boneless
sirloin, 1 inch thick
2 tablespoons vegetable oil
3 stalks celery, cut diagonally into 1/4-inch
slices
2 carrots, cut diagonally into 1/8-inch
slices
1 bunch green onions, cut diagonally into
2-inch pieces
8 ounces mushrooms, thinly sliced (about
4 cups)
1 can (about 8 ounces) bamboo shoots,
drained
4 ounces spinach, stems removed (4 cups)
Hot cooked rice

Dissolve bouillon (dry) in hot water; stir in soy sauce and sugar. Reserve. Cut beef into 1/8-inch slices. (For ease in cutting, partially freeze beef about 1 hour.) Heat oil in 12-inch skillet until hot. Place half each of the celery, carrots, green onions, mushrooms and bamboo shoots in separate areas in skillet. Pour half the reserved soy sauce mixture into skillet.

Simmer uncovered until vegetables are crisp-tender, turning vegetables gently, 8 to 10 minutes. Push vegetables to side of skillet; add half each of the beef and spinach. Cook beef to desired doneness, about 3 minutes. Reserve and keep warm. Repeat with remaining vegetables and beef. Serve with rice.

Swiss Steak

1/4 cup all-purpose flour
1/2 teaspoon salt
1/4 teaspoon pepper
2-pound beef round steak, 1 inch thick
2 tablespoons shortening
1 can (8 ounces) tomatoes
1 medium onion, minced (about 1/2 cup)
1/4 cup minced green pepper
1/2 teaspoon salt
1/8 teaspoon pepper

Mix flour, salt and pepper. Sprinkle one side of meat with half the flour mixture; pound in. Turn meat; pound in remaining flour mixture. Cut meat into 6 serving pieces. Melt shortening in large skillet; add meat and brown over medium heat, about 15 minutes.

Cover tightly; simmer 1 hour. Add small amount of water if necessary. Mix remaining ingredients; pour on meat. Cover tightly; simmer 30 minutes or until tender.

Following pages: Sukiyaki

Dilled Steak with Vegetables

6 SERVINGS

1½-pound lean beef bone-in round or
chuck steak, about ½ inch thick
2 tablespoons all-purpose flour
½ teaspoon salt
⅛ teaspoon pepper
1 tablespoon vegetable oil
½ cup water
2 teaspoons vinegar
½ teaspoon dried dill weed
12 small new potatoes (about 1½ pounds)
3 medium zucchini, cut into 1-inch slices
¼ cup cold water
2 tablespoons all-purpose flour
½ cup plain yogurt

Trim fat from beef steak. Mix 2 tablespoons flour, the salt and pepper. Sprinkle 1 side of beef with half of the flour mixture; pound in. Turn beef and pound in remaining flour mixture. Cut beef into 6 serving pieces. Heat oil in 4-quart Dutch oven. Cook beef in oil over medium heat until brown, about 15 minutes. Mix ½ cup water, the vinegar and dill weed; pour over beef. Heat to boiling; reduce heat. Cover and simmer until beef is just tender, about 45 minutes. Add potatoes; cover and simmer 15 minutes. Add zucchini; cover and simmer until vegetables are tender, 10 to 15 minutes. Remove beef and vegetables; keep warm.

Add enough water to cooking liquid to measure 1 cup. Shake ¼ cup water and 2 tablespoons flour in tightly covered container; gradually stir into cooking liquid. Heat to boiling, stirring constantly. Boil and stir 1 minute. Stir in yogurt; heat just until hot. Serve with beef and vegetables.

Beef with Olives and Almonds

4 SERVINGS

1 pound ground beef
1 medium onion, chopped (about ½ cup)
1 clove garlic, chopped
2 tomatoes, chopped
1 green pepper, chopped
¼ cup raisins
1 teaspoon salt
⅛ teaspoon ground cinnamon
⅛ teaspoon ground cloves
¼ cup slivered almonds
¼ cup sliced pimiento-stuffed olives
Hot cooked rice

Cook and stir beef, onion and garlic in 10-inch skillet until beef is light brown; drain. Add tomatoes, green pepper, raisins, salt, cinnamon and cloves. Cover and simmer 10 minutes.

Cook and stir almonds over medium heat until golden, 2 to 3 minutes. Stir almonds and olives into beef mixture. Serve with rice.

Beef in Pepper Sauce

2 pounds beef boneless sirloin or top loin
    steak, 3/4 inch thick
2 medium red peppers, coarsely chopped
2 jalapeño peppers, seeded and chopped
3 cloves garlic, cut into fourths
1/3 cup dry white wine
1 tablespoon chopped gingerroot
1 1/2 teaspoons salt
1 teaspoon ground turmeric
1/2 teaspoon ground cardamom
1 tablespoon margarine or butter
1 tablespoon vegetable oil
2 medium onions, chopped (about 1 cup)
1 medium red pepper, cut into 1/2-inch
    strips

Trim fat from beef; cut beef across grain into strips, 1 1/2 × 1/2 inch. (For ease in cutting, partially freeze beef about 1 hour.)

Place chopped peppers, jalapeño peppers, garlic, wine, gingerroot, salt, turmeric and cardamom in blender container. Cover and blend on medium-high speed, stopping blender occasionally to scrape sides, until mixed, about 45 seconds.

Heat margarine and oil in 12-inch skillet until hot. Cook and stir beef over medium-high heat until all liquid from beef is evaporated and beef is brown, about 15 minutes; remove beef with slotted spoon. Cook and stir onions and pepper strips in remaining oil mixture over medium heat until tender. Add blended pepper mixture and the beef. Heat to boiling; reduce heat. Simmer uncovered, stirring occasionally, until beef is hot and sauce is slightly thickened, about 10 minutes. Serve with rice or bread, if desired.

Following pages: Beef in Pepper Sauce

Liver and Onions

2 cups thinly sliced onions
3 tablespoons margarine or butter
1 pound liver, sliced ½ to ¾ inch thick
All-purpose flour
¼ cup shortening
Salt and pepper

Cook and stir onions in margarine in 10-inch skillet over medium heat until tender. Remove from skillet; keep warm. Coat liver with flour. Melt shortening in skillet; brown liver over medium-high heat, 2 to 3 minutes on each side, adding onions to skillet during last minute of cooking. Sprinkle with salt and pepper.

Liver Italiano

1 medium onion, sliced
1 tablespoon olive or vegetable oil
1 pound beef liver, about ½ inch thick
2 tablespoons water
1 teaspoon ground coriander
1 teaspoon fennel seed
½ teaspoon salt
½ teaspoon ground cumin
2 cups ¼-inch zucchini or yellow summer
  squash slices (about 2 small)

Cook and stir onion in oil in 10-inch skillet over medium heat until onion is tender, about 5 minutes. Remove onion with slotted spoon; reserve. Cut beef liver into 6 serving pieces if necessary. Cook liver in same skillet over medium-high heat until brown, 2 to 3 minutes on each side. Drizzle water over liver. Mix coriander, fennel, salt and cumin; sprinkle over liver. Arrange onion and zucchini on liver. Cover and cook over low heat until zucchini is crisp-tender, 6 to 8 minutes.

Sweet and Sour Ham

1 can (15¼ ounces) pineapple chunks in
   juice
1 medium onion, sliced
2 tablespoons margarine or butter
1 pound fully cooked smoked ham, cut
   into strips, 4 × ¼ inch
1 small green pepper, chopped (about
   ½ cup)
¼ teaspoon salt
¼ teaspoon pepper
1 tablespoon cornstarch
2 tablespoons cold water
4 cups hot cooked rice

Drain pineapple; reserve juice. Add enough water to juice to measure 1 cup. Cook and stir onion in margarine in 10-inch skillet over medium heat until onion is tender, about 5 minutes. Stir in ham, green pepper, salt, pepper, pineapple chunks and reserved pineapple juice. Heat to boiling; reduce heat. Cover and simmer until green pepper is crisp-tender, about 5 minutes. Mix cornstarch and cold water; gradually stir into ham mixture. Heat to boiling, stirring constantly. Boil and stir 1 minute. Serve over rice.

Pork Chops with Brussels Sprouts

4 pork loin or rib chops, about ½ inch
   thick
2 tablespoons margarine or butter
½ package (24-ounce size) frozen home-
   style potato wedges
1 green or red pepper, chopped
½ pound fresh Brussels sprouts
½ cup dry white wine or apple juice
½ cup water
1½ teaspoons snipped fresh basil leaves
   or ½ teaspoon dried basil leaves
1 teaspoon garlic salt
¼ teaspoon pepper
2 teaspoons cornstarch
2 teaspoons water

Cook pork chops in margarine in 10-inch skillet over medium heat until brown on both sides. Remove pork; keep warm. Cook potatoes and green pepper in skillet, stirring occasionally, until potatoes are light brown, about 6 minutes.

Return pork to skillet; place Brussels sprouts on pork. Add wine, ½ cup water, the basil, garlic salt and pepper. Heat to boiling; reduce heat. Cover and simmer until pork is done and vegetables are tender, about 15 minutes. Remove pork; keep warm.

Mix cornstarch and 2 teaspoons water; stir into vegetables in skillet. Heat to boiling, stirring constantly. Boil and stir 1 minute. Serve vegetables with pork.

Ham and Zucchini with Poppy Seed

6 SERVINGS

1 medium onion, thinly sliced
2 tablespoons margarine or butter
3 cups cut-up fully cooked smoked ham
4 small zucchini (about 1 pound), cut into
    1/4-inch strips
1 green pepper, cut into 1/4-inch slices
1/8 teaspoon pepper
1/2 cup dairy sour cream
1 teaspoon poppy seed

Cook and stir onion in margarine in 10-inch skillet until tender. Stir in ham, zucchini, green pepper and pepper. Cover and cook over medium heat, stirring occasionally, until vegetables are crisp-tender, about 8 minutes.

Stir in sour cream and poppy seed; heat just until hot. Serve with hot cooked rice or noodles, if desired.

Pork Chops in Radish Sauce

6 SERVINGS

Radish and Cilantro Relish (below)
2 tablespoons vegetable oil
6 pork loin or rib chops, about 1/2 inch
    thick
1 teaspoon salt
1/4 teaspoon pepper
2 medium tomatoes, chopped (about
    2 cups)
Hot cooked rice

Prepare Radish and Cilantro Relish; reserve. Heat oil in 10-inch skillet until hot. Cook pork chops in oil over medium heat until brown; sprinkle with salt and pepper. Remove pork from skillet.

Cook and stir relish and tomatoes in same skillet 5 minutes. Add pork. Heat to boiling; reduce heat. Cover and simmer until pork is done, about 45 minutes. Serve with rice. Garnish with snipped fresh cilantro, if desired.

RADISH AND CILANTRO RELISH

2 cups thinly sliced radishes (about 24)
1 medium onion, chopped (about 1/2 cup)
3 tablespoons orange juice
2 tablespoons lime juice
2 tablespoons finely snipped fresh cilantro
2 tablespoons vegetable oil
1/4 teaspoon salt
1/8 teaspoon freshly ground pepper

Mix all ingredients in glass or plastic bowl. Cover and refrigerate at least 1 hour. Makes 3 cups.

Mexican Pork Chops

4 pork loin or rib chops, 1 inch thick
1 teaspoon salt
⅛ teaspoon pepper
1 medium green pepper, cut into 4 rings
4 tablespoons uncooked instant rice
1 can (about 16 ounces) stewed tomatoes

Brown meat over medium heat. Season with salt and pepper. Top each chop with a green pepper ring; fill each ring with 1 tablespoon rice. Carefully pour ¼ cup stewed tomatoes on rice in each ring. Pour remaining tomatoes into skillet. Cover tightly; simmer 1 hour or until done. Add a small amount of water if necessary.

Stir-fried Pork and Pasta

1¼ pounds pork boneless loin or leg
1 teaspoon cornstarch
1 teaspoon soy sauce
¼ teaspoon salt
⅛ teaspoon pepper
2 tablespoons vegetable oil
2 large cloves garlic, finely chopped
¼ to ½ teaspoon finely crushed dried red pepper
2 medium stalks celery, diagonally cut into ¼-inch slices (about 1 cup)
1 small green pepper, cut into 1-inch pieces
2 cups bean sprouts (about 4 ounces)
4 ounces mushrooms, sliced (about 1¼ cups)
2 cups cooked vermicelli (about 4 ounces uncooked)
3 green onions (with tops), sliced
1 tablespoon soy sauce

Trim fat from pork. Cut pork into strips, 2 × 1 × ⅛ inch. Toss pork, cornstarch, 1 teaspoon soy sauce, the salt and pepper. Cover and refrigerate 20 minutes.

Heat oil in 12-inch skillet or wok over high heat until hot. Add pork, garlic and red pepper; cook and stir until pork is no longer pink, about 5 minutes. Add celery and green pepper; cook and stir 2 minutes. Add bean sprouts and mushrooms; cook and stir 2 minutes. Add vermicelli, green onions and 1 tablespoon soy sauce; toss until thoroughly mixed, about 2 minutes.

Following pages: Stir-fried Pork and Pasta

Szechuan Pork

1 pound pork boneless loin or leg
1 tablespoon soy sauce
2 teaspoons cornstarch
1/2 teaspoon ground red pepper
1 clove garlic, finely chopped
2 tablespoons vegetable oil
3 cups broccoli flowerets or 1 package
   (16 ounces) frozen chopped broccoli,
   thawed
2 small onions, cut into eighths
1 can (8 ounces) whole water chestnuts,
   drained
1/4 cup chicken broth
1/2 cup peanuts
Hot cooked rice

Cut pork into slices, 2 × 1 × 1/8 inch. Toss pork, soy sauce, cornstarch, red pepper and garlic in glass or plastic bowl. Cover and refrigerate 20 minutes.

Heat 12-inch skillet or wok until 1 or 2 drops of water bubble and skitter when sprinkled in skillet. Add oil; rotate skillet to coat bottom. Add pork; cook and stir until no longer pink. Add broccoli, onions and water chestnuts; cook and stir 2 minutes. Stir in broth; heat to boiling. Stir in peanuts. Serve with rice.

TO MICROWAVE: Increase cornstarch to 1 tablespoon. Omit oil. Cut pork as directed above. Toss pork, soy sauce, cornstarch, red pepper and garlic in 3-quart microwavable casserole. Cover tightly and refrigerate 20 minutes. Microwave tightly covered on high 4 minutes; stir. Cover tightly and microwave until no longer pink, 5 to 6 minutes longer.

Stir in broccoli, onions, water chestnuts and broth. Cover tightly and microwave 3 minutes; stir. Cover tightly and microwave until broccoli is crisp-tender, 3 to 4 minutes longer. Stir in peanuts. Serve with rice.

Pork and Sauerkraut Dinner

4 pork blade steaks, about 1/2 inch thick
1/4 teaspoon salt
1/8 teaspoon pepper
1 medium onion, thinly sliced
1 can (16 ounces) sauerkraut, drained
1 cup dry white wine
1 teaspoon paprika
2 cloves garlic, crushed

Cook pork in 10-inch skillet over medium heat until brown on both sides; drain. Sprinkle with salt and pepper; reduce heat. Place onion and sauerkraut over pork. Mix wine, paprika and garlic; pour over sauerkraut. Cover and simmer until pork is tender, about 35 minutes.

Pork Chops with Knackwurst

4 pork loin or rib chops, about ½ inch
   thick
1 tablespoon vegetable oil
1 medium onion, chopped (about ½ cup)
1 medium carrot, chopped
1 stalk celery, sliced
2 sweet pickles, finely chopped
6 ounces knackwurst, cut into ¼-inch
   slices
2 teaspoons caraway seed
½ teaspoon salt
½ teaspoon pepper
¾ cup water
3 medium potatoes, cut into ⅛-inch slices

Trim excess fat from pork. Heat oil in 10-inch skillet until hot. Cook pork over medium heat until brown on both sides, about 15 minutes; remove pork.

Cook and stir onion, carrot, celery, pickles and knackwurst in skillet until onion is tender, about 5 minutes. Arrange pork on vegetable mixture; sprinkle with caraway seed, salt and pepper. Pour water over pork. Arrange potato slices on top. Heat to boiling; reduce heat. Cover and simmer until pork and potatoes are tender, about 45 minutes. Garnish with snipped parsley or chives, if desired.

Braised Knackwurst Dinner

2 cups water
2 teaspoons instant beef bouillon
2 large potatoes, cut lengthwise into
   fourths
4 medium carrots, cut into 3 × ½-inch
   strips
2 large onions, cut into fourths
½ medium head cabbage, cut into
   4 wedges
1 teaspoon salt
1 medium apple, cut into wedges
4 to 6 knackwurst
Prepared mustard
Prepared horseradish

Heat water and bouillon (dry) to boiling in 4-quart Dutch oven. Layer potatoes, carrots, onions and cabbage in bouillon; sprinkle with salt. Layer apple and knackwurst on top. Heat to boiling; reduce heat. Cover and simmer until vegetables are tender, 25 to 30 minutes.

Remove knackwurst, apple and vegetables with slotted spoon. Serve with mustard and horseradish.

· 3 ·

CASSEROLES

Beef and Corn Casserole

1/2 small green pepper, chopped (about
   1/4 cup)
1 small onion, chopped (about 1/4 cup)
1 tablespoon margarine or butter
2 packages (2 1/2 ounces each) thinly sliced
   smoked beef, chopped
1 cup sliced mushrooms
1/4 cup margarine or butter
1/4 cup all-purpose flour
1/2 teaspoon salt
1/4 teaspoon pepper
2 cups milk
2 egg yolks, slightly beaten
1 teaspoon prepared mustard
1 can (17 ounces) whole kernel corn,
   drained
1/3 cup dry bread crumbs
1/4 cup grated Parmesan cheese
2 tablespoons margarine or butter, melted
1/4 teaspoon paprika

Cook and stir green pepper and onion in 1 tablespoon margarine in 10-inch skillet until onion is tender. Add beef and mushrooms; cook and stir until edges of beef curl.

Heat 1/4 cup margarine in 1-quart saucepan over low heat until melted. Stir in flour, salt and pepper. Cook, stirring constantly, until smooth and bubbly; remove from heat. Stir in milk. Heat to boiling, stirring constantly. Boil and stir 1 minute. Stir at least half of the hot mixture gradually into egg yolks. Blend into hot mixture in saucepan. Boil and stir 1 minute; stir in mustard. Stir sauce and corn into beef mixture.

OVEN METHOD: Pour into ungreased 1 1/2-quart casserole or 10 × 6 × 1 1/2-inch baking dish. Mix remaining ingredients; sprinkle over beef mixture. Cook uncovered in 350° oven until hot and bubbly, about 30 minutes.

RANGE-TOP METHOD: Heat to boiling; reduce heat. Simmer uncovered, stirring occasionally, until hot, 5 to 8 minutes; remove from heat. Mix remaining ingredients; sprinkle over beef mixture.

African Beef and Rice

1-pound beef round steak, 1/2 inch thick
2 tablespoons vegetable oil
1 cup water
1 bay leaf
1 teaspoon salt
1/8 to 1/4 teaspoon crushed red pepper
1 can (16 ounces) red kidney beans,
   drained
1 cup uncooked regular rice
2 medium green peppers, cut into 1-inch
   pieces
1 medium onion, chopped (about 1/2 cup)
1 1/2 teaspoons salt
1/2 to 1 teaspoon curry powder
1/4 teaspoon pepper

Cut beef into 1-inch pieces. Heat oil in 10-inch skillet until hot. Cook and stir beef in oil over medium heat until brown on all sides, about 15 minutes. Add water, bay leaf, 1 teaspoon salt and the red pepper. Heat to boiling; reduce heat. Cover and simmer 45 minutes.

Drain beef, reserving broth. Add enough water to reserved broth to measure 2 cups. Mix beef, broth and remaining ingredients. Pour into ungreased 2-quart casserole. Cover and cook in 350° oven until liquid is absorbed, 45 to 50 minutes. Serve with sliced tomatoes, if desired.

Beef Burgundy

2 1/2 pounds beef boneless chuck, tip or
   round (1 to 1 1/4 inches thick)
1/4 cup vegetable oil
3 tablespoons all-purpose flour
1 1/2 teaspoons salt
2 teaspoons instant beef bouillon
1/4 teaspoon dried marjoram leaves
1/4 teaspoon dried thyme leaves
1/8 teaspoon pepper
1 1/4 cups red Burgundy or other dry red
   wine
3/4 cup water
5 medium onions, sliced, or 12 small
   whole onions
8 ounces mushrooms, cut into halves
Snipped parsley

Cut beef lengthwise into 1/4-inch strips; cut strips into 2- to 3-inch pieces. (For easier cutting, partially freeze beef.) Cook and stir beef in oil in 4-quart Dutch oven over medium heat until brown; drain. Sprinkle beef with flour, salt, bouillon (dry), marjoram, thyme and pepper. Stir in Burgundy, water and onions.

OVEN METHOD: Cover and cook in 325° oven until beef is tender, about 1 1/2 hours. Stir in mushrooms. Cover and cook until mushrooms are done, 10 to 15 minutes. Sprinkle with parsley.

RANGE-TOP METHOD: Heat to boiling; reduce heat. Cover and simmer until beef is tender, about 1 hour. Stir in mushrooms. Cover and simmer until mushrooms are done, 10 to 15 minutes. Sprinkle with parsley.

Hearty Beef Casserole

7 SERVINGS

1½ pounds ground beef
1 large onion, chopped (about 1 cup)
2 medium tomatoes, chopped (about 2 cups)
2 cups water
1 cup uncooked bulgur
3 tablespoons snipped parsley
2 teaspoons instant beef bouillon
1½ teaspoons salt
½ teaspoon dried oregano leaves
¼ teaspoon instant minced garlic
¼ teaspoon pepper
½ cup grated Parmesan cheese

Cook and stir ground beef and onion in 10-inch skillet until beef is brown; drain. Stir in remaining ingredients except cheese.

OVEN METHOD: Pour into ungreased 2-quart casserole or $12 \times 7\frac{1}{2} \times 2$-inch baking dish. Cover and cook in 350° oven until wheat is tender, about 45 minutes. Stir in cheese. Sprinkle with additional Parmesan cheese and snipped parsley, if desired.

RANGE-TOP METHOD: Heat to boiling; reduce heat. Cover and simmer, stirring occasionally, until wheat is tender, about 30 minutes. (Add small amount water if necessary.) Stir in cheese. Sprinkle with additional Parmesan cheese and snipped parsley, if desired.

TO MICROWAVE: Crumble ground beef into 3-quart microwavable casserole; add onion. Cover loosely and microwave on high 5 minutes; break up and stir. Cover and microwave until very little pink remains, 4 to 6 minutes longer; drain. Stir in remaining ingredients except cheese. Cover tightly and microwave 10 minutes; stir. Cover and microwave until wheat is tender, 10 to 14 minutes longer. Stir in cheese. Sprinkle with additional Parmesan cheese and snipped parsley, if desired.

Beef and Eggplant Casserole

6 TO 8 SERVINGS

1 pound ground beef
1 small eggplant (about 1 pound), cut into
    1-inch pieces (about 5 cups)
1 cup uncooked elbow spaghetti (about
    3 ounces)
1/2 cup water
1 clove garlic, finely chopped
1 tablespoon salt
1 teaspoon dried oregano leaves
1/4 teaspoon pepper
4 medium tomatoes, each cut into fourths
2 medium onions, coarsely chopped (about
    2 cups)
1 medium green pepper, cut into strips
1/4 cup grated Parmesan cheese

Cook and stir ground beef in 4-quart Dutch oven until brown; drain. Stir in eggplant, spaghetti, water, garlic, salt, oregano and pepper.

OVEN METHOD: Pour into ungreased 3-quart casserole or 13 × 9 × 2-inch baking dish. Top with tomatoes, onions and green pepper. Cover and cook in 350° oven until eggplant is tender, 50 to 60 minutes. Stir; sprinkle with cheese. Serve with additional Parmesan cheese, if desired.

RANGE-TOP METHOD: Heat to boiling, stirring constantly; reduce heat. Top with tomatoes, onions and green pepper. Cover and simmer, stirring occasionally, until spaghetti is tender and vegetables are crisp-tender, 20 to 25 minutes. Stir; sprinkle with cheese. Serve with additional Parmesan cheese, if desired.

Following pages: African Beef and Rice, left, (page 39) and Beef and Eggplant Casserole, right

Green Bean and Mushroom Casserole

1 pound ground beef
1 medium onion, chopped (about ½ cup)
1 can (16 ounces) green beans
1 can (10¾ ounces) condensed cream of
mushroom soup
1 can (4 ounces) mushroom stems and
pieces, drained
1 small green pepper, chopped (about
½ cup)
1 medium stalk celery, chopped (about
½ cup)
1 cup milk
1 tablespoon Worcestershire sauce
1 teaspoon salt
2 cups uncooked egg noodles

Cook and stir ground beef and onion in 12-inch skillet or 4-quart Dutch oven until beef is brown; drain. Stir in beans (with liquid) and the remaining ingredients.

OVEN METHOD: Pour into ungreased 2-quart casserole or 12 × 7½ × 2-inch baking dish. Cover and cook in 350° oven until noodles are tender, about 35 minutes.

RANGE-TOP METHOD: Heat to boiling; reduce heat. Cover and simmer, stirring occasionally, until noodles are tender, 25 to 30 minutes.

TO MICROWAVE: Crumble ground beef into 3-quart microwavable casserole; add onion. Cover loosely and microwave on high 3 minutes; break up and stir. Cover and microwave until very little pink remains, 2 to 3 minutes longer; drain. Stir in beans (with liquid) and the remaining ingredients. Cover tightly and microwave 8 minutes; stir. Cover and microwave until noodles are almost tender, 8 to 12 minutes longer; stir. Cover and let stand 5 minutes.

GREEN BEAN–TOMATO CASSEROLE: Omit mushrooms and milk. Stir in 1 can (28 ounces) whole tomatoes (with liquid) and ½ cup ketchup with the remaining ingredients.

Meatballs with Mixed Vegetables

1 package (10 ounces) frozen mixed
  vegetables
1 egg
1/4 cup milk
1 cup soft bread crumbs
1/2 teaspoon salt
1/2 teaspoon dry mustard
1/2 teaspoon celery salt
1/4 teaspoon ground nutmeg
1/4 teaspoon pepper
3 teaspoons grated onion
1 pound ground beef
2 tablespoons shortening
1 can (10¾ ounces) condensed cream of
  mushroom soup
¾ cup milk

Rinse frozen vegetables under running cold water to separate; drain. Mix egg, milk, bread crumbs, salt, mustard, celery salt, nutmeg, pepper, onion and ground beef. Shape into about 1½-inch balls. Heat shortening in 10-inch skillet until melted. Cook meatballs in shortening until done; drain.

OVEN METHOD: Place meatballs in ungreased 1½-quart casserole or 10 × 6 × 1½-inch baking dish. Mix vegetables, soup and milk. Pour over meatballs; stir. Cover and cook in 350° oven until vegetables are tender, 25 to 30 minutes.

RANGE-TOP METHOD: Remove meatballs from skillet. Mix vegetables, soup and milk in skillet. Heat to boiling; reduce heat. Cover and simmer until vegetables are tender, 10 to 15 minutes. Add meatballs; heat through.

TO MICROWAVE: Place meatballs in 8 × 8 × 2-inch microwavable baking dish. Cover loosely and microwave on high 4 minutes; rearrange meatballs. Cover and microwave 4 minutes; drain. Mix vegetables, soup and milk; pour over meatballs. Cover tightly and microwave until meatballs are done and vegetables are tender, 5 to 8 minutes longer.

Beef and Potato Strata

2 1/2 cups water
1 package (5.5 ounces) au gratin potato
  mix
2 pounds ground beef
1 medium onion, chopped (about 1/2 cup)
1 can (16 ounces) whole tomatoes
1 can (8 ounces) tomato sauce or pizza
  sauce
1/2 teaspoon salt
1 teaspoon dried oregano leaves
1/2 teaspoon dried basil leaves
1/8 teaspoon garlic powder
1 cup creamed cottage cheese (small curd)
2 cups shredded mozzarella cheese (about
  8 ounces)
1/2 cup grated Parmesan cheese

Heat water to boiling; add potatoes. Cook until water is absorbed. Cook and stir ground beef and onion in 10-inch skillet until beef is brown; drain. Stir in Sauce Mix, tomatoes (with liquid), tomato sauce, salt, oregano, basil and garlic powder; break up tomatoes. Simmer uncovered 20 minutes.

Reserve 1 cup beef mixture. Spread 1 cup of the remaining beef mixture in greased 13 × 9 × 2-inch baking dish. Top with half of the potatoes, half of the remaining beef mixture, 1/2 cup of the cottage cheese, 1 cup mozzarella cheese and 1/4 cup of the Parmesan cheese. Repeat with remaining potatoes, beef mixture, cottage cheese and mozzarella cheese. Spread reserved beef mixture over top. Sprinkle with remaining Parmesan cheese. Cook uncovered in 350° oven 30 minutes. Let stand 10 minutes before cutting.

Broccoli-Beef Bake

2 cups chopped fresh broccoli*
1 pound ground beef
1 can (4 ounces) mushroom stems and
    pieces, drained
2 cups shredded Cheddar cheese (about
    8 ounces)
1/3 cup chopped onion
2 cups variety baking mix
1/2 cup cold water
1/4 cup grated Parmesan cheese
1 teaspoon salt
Dash of pepper
1/2 cup milk
4 eggs

Heat 1 inch salted water (1/2 teaspoon salt to 1 cup water) to boiling. Add broccoli. Cover and heat to boiling. Cook until almost tender, about 5 minutes; drain thoroughly.

Cook and stir ground beef in 10-inch skillet until brown; drain. Stir in mushrooms, 1 1/2 cups of the Cheddar cheese and the onion. Mix baking mix, water and the remaining Cheddar cheese until soft dough forms; beat vigorously 20 strokes. Pat dough in greased 13 × 9 × 2-inch baking dish with floured hands, pressing dough 1/2 inch up sides. Spread beef mixture over dough; sprinkle with broccoli. Mix remaining ingredients; pour over broccoli. Cook uncovered in 400° oven until golden brown and knife inserted near center comes out clean, 25 to 30 minutes.

*1 package (10 ounces) frozen chopped broccoli, thawed and drained, can be substituted for the fresh broccoli. Do not cook.

Following pages: Broccoli-Beef Bake, left, and Beef and Potato Strata, right

Pork with Coriander

5 SERVINGS

2 *pounds pork boneless shoulder*
1 *tablespoon vegetable oil*
1 *cup dry white wine*
1 *tablespoon ground coriander*
1 *teaspoon salt*
1 *pound new potatoes, cut into halves*
8 *ounces mushrooms, cut into halves*

Trim fat from pork; cut pork into 1-inch cubes. Heat oil in Dutch oven until hot. Cook pork over medium heat, stirring occasionally, until all liquid is evaporated and pork is brown, about 25 minutes; drain fat.

Stir in wine, coriander and salt. Heat to boiling; reduce heat. Cover and simmer 45 minutes. Stir in potatoes and mushrooms. Heat to boiling; reduce heat. Cover and simmer until pork and potatoes are tender, 15 to 20 minutes. Serve with wheat pilaf and tossed green salad if desired.

Pork Chop and Potato Casserole

6 SERVINGS

6 *pork loin or rib chops,* ¹/₂ *inch thick*
2 *tablespoons vegetable oil*
1 *can (10³/₄ ounces) condensed cream of*
  mushroom soup
1 *can (4 ounces) mushroom stems and*
  pieces
¹/₄ *cup water*
¹/₂ *teaspoon garlic salt*
¹/₄ *teaspoon dried thyme leaves*
2 *tablespoons dry white wine*
¹/₂ *teaspoon Worcestershire sauce*
1 *tablespoon chopped pimiento*
1 *can (16 ounces) whole potatoes, drained*
1 *package (10 ounces) frozen green peas,*
  rinsed and drained

Cook pork in oil in 10-inch skillet over medium-high heat until brown on both sides.

OVEN METHOD: Place pork in ungreased 13 × 9 × 2-inch pan. Mix soup, mushrooms (with liquid), water, garlic salt, thyme, wine and Worcestershire sauce; pour over pork. Cover and cook in 350° oven 1 hour. Stir in pimiento, potatoes and peas. Cover and cook until peas are tender and potatoes are hot, about 15 minutes.

RANGE-TOP METHOD: Mix soup, mushrooms (with liquid), water, garlic salt, thyme, wine and Worcestershire sauce; pour over pork. Heat to boiling, stirring occasionally; reduce heat. Cover and simmer 30 minutes. Stir in pimiento, potatoes and peas. Cover and simmer, stirring occasionally, until peas are tender and potatoes are hot, about 10 minutes.

Sausage and Vegetable Popover

4 precooked Polish sausages (about
   1 pound), sliced
1 can (4 ounces) chopped green chilies,
   drained
1½ teaspoons chili powder
1 teaspoon dried oregano leaves
½ teaspoon seasoned salt
½ teaspoon ground cumin
½ teaspoon garlic salt
½ teaspoon sugar
1 tablespoon vegetable oil
1 can (11 ounces) whole kernel corn with
   sweet peppers, drained
1 can (4 ounces) mushroom stems and
   pieces, drained
1 tablespoon margarine or butter
2 eggs
¾ cup all-purpose flour
¾ cup milk
1 cup shredded Monterey Jack or
   Cheddar cheese (about 4 ounces)
2 green onions (with tops), chopped

Cook and stir sausages, chilies, chili powder, oregano, seasoned salt, cumin, garlic salt and sugar in oil in 12-inch skillet until sausages are light brown. Stir in corn and mushrooms; keep warm.

Heat oven to 400°. Heat margarine in 9 × 1¼-inch pie plate in oven until melted. Beat eggs, flour and milk until smooth; pour into pie plate. Mound sausage mixture in pie plate to within 1 inch of edge. Cook uncovered 20 minutes; sprinkle with cheese. Cook until cheese is melted, 10 to 15 minutes. Sprinkle with onions.

Following pages: Sausage and Vegetable Popover

Pork Sausage and Bean Casserole

1 pound bulk pork sausage
2 medium stalks celery, sliced
1 medium onion, chopped (about ½ cup)
1 large clove garlic, crushed
*2 cans (16 ounces each) baked beans in
  tomato sauce*
1 can (17 ounces) lima beans, drained
1 can (15½ ounces) kidney beans, drained
1 can (8 ounces) tomato sauce
1 tablespoon dry mustard
2 tablespoons honey
1 tablespoon vinegar
1 teaspoon salt
¼ teaspoon red pepper sauce

Cook and stir sausage, celery, onion and garlic until sausage is brown, about 10 minutes; drain. Mix sausage mixture and remaining ingredients in ungreased 3-quart casserole.

Bake uncovered in 400° oven, stirring once, until hot and bubbly, about 45 minutes.

TO MICROWAVE: Place sausage, celery, onion and garlic in 3-quart microwavable casserole. Cover tightly and microwave on high 4 minutes; stir. Cover tightly and microwave until sausage is no longer pink, 2 to 5 minutes longer; drain.

Mix sausage mixture and remaining ingredients in same casserole. Cover tightly and microwave 10 minutes; stir. Cover tightly and microwave on medium (50%) to blend flavors, 15 minutes.

Canadian-style Bacon and Zucchini

8 SERVINGS

2 eggs
2 cups creamed cottage cheese
¾ cup uncooked instant rice
1 medium onion, chopped (about ½ cup)
2 tablespoons snipped parsley
1½ teaspoons dried marjoram leaves
¾ teaspoon salt
Few drops red pepper sauce
2 pounds zucchini, cut into ½-inch slices
¾ cup grated Parmesan cheese
*1 pound Canadian-style bacon, cut into
  16 slices*

Beat eggs slightly with fork; stir in cottage cheese, rice, onion, parsley, marjoram, salt and pepper sauce. Arrange half of the zucchini slices in ungreased 2-quart casserole or $12 \times 7½ \times 2$-inch baking dish. Cover with half of the cheese-rice mixture. Repeat with remaining zucchini and cheese-rice mixture; sprinkle with Parmesan cheese. Overlap bacon slices on top. Cook uncovered in 350° oven until golden brown, about 1 hour.

Ham and Eggplant Au Gratin

1/4 cup margarine or butter
1/4 cup all-purpose flour
1 teaspoon dry mustard
1/2 teaspoon salt
1/4 teaspoon pepper
1/4 teaspoon paprika
2 cups milk
1 jar (5 ounces) pimiento cheese spread
1 small onion, chopped (about 1/4 cup)
1 medium eggplant, cut into 1/2-inch cubes
2 cups cut-up fully cooked smoked ham
2 medium tomatoes, cut into 1/2-inch slices
1/2 cup bread crumbs

Heat 1/4 cup margarine in 2-quart saucepan over low heat until melted. Stir in flour, mustard, salt, pepper and paprika. Cook, stirring constantly, until smooth and bubbly; remove from heat. Stir in milk. Heat to boiling, stirring constantly. Boil and stir 1 minute. Stir in cheese spread and onion. Heat over low heat, stirring occasionally, until cheese is melted.

Layer half each of the eggplant, ham and cheese sauce in ungreased 12 × 7½ × 2-inch baking dish; repeat. Top with tomatoes; sprinkle bread crumbs over tomatoes. Cook uncovered in 350° oven until hot and bubbly, 25 to 30 minutes.

Lamb Casserole

2 small onions, thinly sliced
1/4 cup vegetable oil
1 pound lamb for stew, cut into 1/2-inch pieces
1 small eggplant (about 1 pound), cut crosswise into slices
Salt and pepper
1 can (8 ounces) cut green beans, drained
2 medium carrots, sliced
1 large green pepper, cut into rings
4 medium tomatoes, cut into 1/2-inch slices
2 cups cooked rice
1 cup shredded Cheddar cheese (about 4 ounces)
Paprika
2 tablespoons snipped parsley

Cook and stir onions in oil in 10-inch skillet until onions are tender; remove from skillet. Cook and stir lamb in same skillet until brown; drain.

Arrange eggplant slices in ungreased 13 × 9 × 2-inch baking dish; top with lamb. Sprinkle with salt and pepper. Layer onions, beans, carrots, green pepper and tomatoes on lamb. Sprinkle with salt and pepper. Cover and cook until lamb is tender, about 1 hour.

Arrange rice by 1/2 cupfuls in 4 diagonal strips on casserole. Top rice with cheese; sprinkle with paprika. Cook uncovered until cheese is melted, 15 to 20 minutes. Sprinkle with parsley.

· 4 ·

SOUPS AND STEWS

African Beef and Vegetable Soup

6 SERVINGS

1½ pounds beef boneless chuck, tip or round, cut into ¾-inch cubes
2 cups water
2 teaspoons salt
¼ teaspoon ground ginger
⅛ to ¼ teaspoon ground red pepper
1½ pounds Hubbard squash, pared and cut into 1-inch cubes*
2 medium tomatoes, chopped
1 package (10 ounces) frozen baby lima beans

Heat beef, water, salt, ginger and red pepper to boiling in Dutch oven; reduce heat. Cover and simmer 1½ hours. Add squash; cover and cook until beef and squash are tender, 30 to 45 minutes longer.

Remove squash; mash or puree in blender. Return squash to Dutch oven. Add tomatoes and beans. Heat to boiling; reduce heat. Cover and simmer until beans are tender, about 15 minutes. Top each serving with hot cooked rice, if desired.

*1 package (12 ounces) frozen cooked squash, thawed, can be substituted for the fresh squash; add with tomatoes.

Russian Beet Soup

6 cups water
4 ounces dried navy beans (about 1/2 cup)
1 pound beef boneless chuck, tip or round,
   cut into 1/2-inch cubes
1 smoked pork hock
1 can (10 1/2 ounces) condensed beef broth
2 1/2 teaspoons salt
1/4 teaspoon pepper
6 medium beets, cooked
2 medium onions, sliced
2 cloves garlic, chopped
2 medium potatoes, cut into 1/2-inch cubes
3 cups shredded cabbage
2 teaspoons dill seed or 1 sprig dill weed
1 tablespoon pickling spice
1/4 cup red wine vinegar
1 cup dairy sour cream

Heat water and beans to boiling in Dutch oven; boil 2 minutes. Remove from heat; cover and let stand 1 hour. Add beef, pork, beef broth, salt and pepper to beans. Heat to boiling; reduce heat. Cover and simmer until beef is tender, 1 to 1 1/2 hours. Shred beets or cut into 1/4-inch strips.

Remove pork from Dutch oven; cool slightly. Remove pork from bone and trim fat; cut into bite-size pieces. Add pork, beets, onions, garlic, potatoes and cabbage to beef mixture. Tie dill seed and pickling spice in cheesecloth bag or place in tea ball; add to beef mixture. Cover and simmer 2 hours. Stir in vinegar; simmer 10 minutes. Remove spice bag. Serve with sour cream; sprinkle with snipped dill weed, if desired.

Scotch Broth

1 1/2 pounds lamb boneless shoulder
6 cups water
1/2 cup barley
2 teaspoons salt
1/2 teaspoon pepper
3 carrots, sliced
2 stalks celery, sliced
2 medium onions, chopped (about 1 cup)
1 cup diced rutabaga or turnip
Snipped parsley

Trim fat from lamb; cut lamb into 3/4-inch cubes. Heat lamb, water, barley, salt and pepper to boiling in Dutch oven; reduce heat. Cover and simmer 1 hour.

Add vegetables to lamb mixture. Cover and simmer until lamb and vegetables are tender, about 30 minutes. Skim fat if necessary. Sprinkle with parsley.

Following pages: Russian Beet Soup, left, and Southwest Black Bean Soup, right (page 60)

Southwest Black Bean Soup

1 large onion, chopped (about 1 cup)
4 cloves garlic, finely chopped
2 tablespoons vegetable oil
1 pound dried black beans
2 cups cubed fully cooked smoked ham
6 cups chicken broth
2 tablespoons ground red chilies
2 tablespoons snipped fresh cilantro
1 tablespoon dried oregano leaves
2 teaspoons ground cumin
1 can (28 ounces) whole tomatoes, undrained
1 canned chipotle chili in adobo sauce
Quick Crème Fraîche (below)
Chopped red bell pepper

Cook and stir onion and garlic in oil in 4-quart Dutch oven until onion is tender. Stir in remaining ingredients except Quick Crème Fraîche and bell pepper; heat to boiling. Boil 2 minutes; reduce heat. Cover and simmer until beans are tender, about 2¼ hours.

Pour ¼ of the soup into food processor workbowl fitted with steel blade or into blender container; cover and process until smooth. Repeat with remaining soup. Serve with Quick Crème Fraîche and bell pepper.

QUICK CRÈME FRAÎCHE

⅓ cup whipping cream
⅔ cup dairy sour cream

Gradually stir whipping cream into sour cream. Cover and refrigerate up to 48 hours.

Sausage-Bean Soup

6 SERVINGS

1 pound fully cooked smoked kielbasa, cut
  into ¼-inch slices
1 medium onion, chopped (about ½ cup)
1 medium green pepper, chopped (about
  1 cup)
⅔ cup uncooked regular rice
1½ cups water
1 can (28 ounces) whole tomatoes,
  undrained
1 can (10½ ounces) condensed beef broth
1 teaspoon dried oregano leaves
¼ teaspoon pepper
1 can (16 ounces) red kidney beans,
  drained

Cook and stir kielbasa and onion in 4-quart
Dutch oven over medium heat until onion is
tender, about 10 minutes. Stir in remaining
ingredients except beans; break up tomatoes.
Heat to boiling; reduce heat. Cover and simmer 30 minutes. Stir in beans. Heat, stirring
occasionally, just until beans are hot, about 5
minutes.

Easy Burgundy Stew

8 SERVINGS

2 pounds beef boneless bottom or top
  round, tip or chuck steak, cut into
  1-inch cubes
4 medium carrots, sliced (about 2 cups)
2 medium stalks celery, sliced (about
  1 cup)
2 medium onions, sliced
1 can (8 ounces) water chestnuts, sliced
1 can (8 ounces) mushroom stems and
  pieces, drained
3 tablespoons all-purpose flour
1 teaspoon salt
1 teaspoon dried thyme leaves
1 teaspoon dry mustard
¼ teaspoon pepper
1 can (16 ounces) whole tomatoes,
  undrained
1 cup water
1 cup dry red wine

Mix beef, carrots, celery, onions, water chestnuts and mushrooms in 4-quart Dutch oven
or casserole. Mix flour, salt, thyme, mustard
and pepper; stir into beef mixture. Stir in
remaining ingredients; break up tomatoes.
Cover and cook in 325° oven until beef is
tender and stew is thickened, about 4 hours.

PRESSURE COOKER DIRECTIONS: Increase flour
to ⅓ cup and omit 1 cup water. Mix all ingredients in 6-quart pressure cooker. Following manufacturer's directions, cover and cook at 15
pounds pressure 30 minutes. Cool 5 minutes;
reduce pressure. Uncover and cook, stirring
occasionally, until stew is thickened, about 10
minutes.

Note: 1 cup water and 1 teaspoon instant beef
bouillon can be substituted for the wine.

Following pages: Sausage-Bean Soup

SOUPS AND STEWS   61

Hungarian Beef Goulash

2 tablespoons vegetable oil or bacon fat
1½ pounds beef boneless chuck, tip or
    round, cut into ¾-inch cubes
2 cups water
1 can (8 ounces) tomatoes (with liquid)
3 medium onions, chopped (about
    1½ cups)
1 clove garlic, chopped
2 teaspoons paprika
2 teaspoons salt
1 teaspoon instant beef bouillon
½ teaspoon caraway seed
¼ teaspoon pepper
2 medium potatoes, cut into 1½-inch
    pieces
2 medium green peppers, cut into 1-inch
    pieces
French bread or rolls

Heat oil in Dutch oven or 12-inch skillet until hot. Cook and stir beef in hot oil until brown, about 15 minutes; drain. Add water, tomatoes, onions, garlic, paprika, salt, bouillon (dry), caraway seed and pepper; break up tomatoes. Heat to boiling; reduce heat. Cover and simmer 1 hour.

Add potatoes; cover and simmer until beef and potatoes are tender, about 30 minutes. Add green peppers; cover and simmer until tender, 8 to 10 minutes. Serve in soup bowls with French bread for dipping into hot broth.

Oven Stew

2 pounds beef round steak, cut into 1-inch
    cubes
2 cups sliced carrots
1 cup sliced celery
2 medium onions, sliced
1 can (8 ounces) water chestnuts, drained
    and sliced
1 can (4 ounces) sliced mushrooms,
    drained
3 tablespoons flour
1 tablespoon sugar
1 tablespoon salt
1 can (16 ounces) tomatoes
1 cup red Burgundy

Mix meat, carrots, celery, onions, water chestnuts and mushrooms in Dutch oven. Mix flour, sugar and salt; stir into meat mixture. Stir in tomatoes and wine. Cover tightly; cook in 325° oven or on top of range 4 hours.

Note: 1 cup water and 1 teaspoon beef bouillon can be substituted for the Burgundy.

Red Wine Beef Stew

¼ pound salt pork
1½ pounds beef boneless chuck, tip or
  round steak, cut into 1-inch pieces
1 cup dry red wine
½ cup water
½ teaspoon salt
½ teaspoon dried thyme leaves
¼ teaspoon dried rosemary leaves
¼ teaspoon pepper
2 cloves garlic, chopped
1 bay leaf
6 carrots, cut into 1-inch pieces
2 medium onions, cut into fourths
½ cup pitted ripe olives
Snipped parsley

Remove rind from salt pork; cut pork into ¼-inch slices. Cook salt pork in 4-quart Dutch oven over medium heat until crisp. Remove with slotted spoon; drain.

Cook and stir beef in hot fat until brown, about 15 minutes; drain fat. Add wine, water, salt, and seasonings to Dutch oven. Heat to boiling; reduce heat. Cover and simmer 1 hour.

Stir in salt pork, carrots, onions and olives. Cover and simmer until beef and vegetables are tender, about 40 minutes. Remove bay leaf. Sprinkle with parsley.

TO MICROWAVE: Omit water. Cut beef into ½-inch cubes. Place salt pork and beef in 3-quart microwavable casserole. Cover tightly and microwave on high 5 minutes; stir. Cover tightly and microwave until almost no pink remains, 3 to 5 minutes longer. Remove salt pork; reserve.

Add wine, salt and seasonings to beef. Cover tightly and microwave on medium-low (30%) 20 minutes; stir. Cover tightly and microwave 20 minutes longer. Add salt pork, carrots, onions and olives. Cover tightly and microwave on medium (50%) 10 minutes; stir. Cover tightly and microwave until carrots are tender, 10 to 15 minutes longer. Remove bay leaf. Sprinkle with parsley.

Beef Stew Provençale

¹/₄ pound salt pork
1¹/₂ pounds beef boneless chuck, tip or
* round*
1 cup dry red wine
¹/₂ cup water
2 cloves garlic, chopped
¹/₂ teaspoon salt
¹/₂ teaspoon dried thyme leaves
¹/₄ teaspoon dried rosemary leaves,
* crushed*
¹/₄ teaspoon pepper
1 bay leaf
6 medium carrots, cut into 1-inch pieces
2 medium onions, cut into fourths
¹/₂ cup pitted ripe olives
Snipped parsley
French bread

Remove rind from salt pork; cut pork into ¹/₄-inch slices. Cut beef into 1-inch cubes. (For ease in cutting, partially freeze beef about 1 hour.) Fry salt pork in Dutch oven over medium heat until crisp; remove with slotted spoon. Drain on paper towels. Cook and stir beef in hot fat until brown, about 15 minutes. Drain fat. Add wine, water, garlic, salt, thyme, rosemary, pepper and bay leaf. Heat to boiling; reduce heat. Cover and simmer 1 hour.

Stir in salt pork, carrots, onions and olives. Cover and simmer until beef and vegetables are tender, about 40 minutes. Remove bay leaf. Sprinkle with parsley. Serve in bowls with French bread for dipping.

Beef Stew with Chutney

4 SERVINGS

1¹/₂-pound beef boneless chuck, tip or
* round roast, cut into 1-inch pieces*
2 tablespoons olive or vegetable oil
¹/₂ cup chutney
1 cup apple juice or water
1 tablespoon curry powder
2 medium tomatoes, chopped
1 large onion, sliced
1 small butternut squash, cut into cubes
Hot cooked bulgur or rice

Cook and stir beef in oil in 4-quart Dutch oven or 12-inch skillet until brown, about 15 minutes; drain. Stir in remaining ingredients except squash and bulgur. Heat to boiling; reduce heat. Cover and simmer until beef is almost tender, about 2 hours.

Stir in squash; cover and cook until beef and squash are tender, about 15 minutes. Serve with bulgur and, if desired, additional chutney and chopped cilantro.

TO MICROWAVE: Cut beef into ¹/₂-inch pieces. Omit oil; decrease apple juice to ¹/₂ cup and curry powder to 2 teaspoons. Place beef and onion in 3-quart microwavable casserole. Cover

66   BETTY CROCKER'S RED SPOON COLLECTION

tightly and microwave on high 6 minutes; stir. Cover tightly and microwave until beef is no longer pink, 6 to 8 minutes longer (do not drain).

Stir in remaining ingredients except squash, bulgur and cilantro. Cover tightly and microwave to boiling, 4 to 6 minutes; stir. Cover tightly and microwave on medium-low (30%) 15 minutes; stir. Cover tightly and microwave 15 minutes longer. Stir in squash. Cover tightly and microwave until beef and squash are tender, 15 to 20 minutes. Serve as directed above.

Beef and Plantains

6 TO 8 SERVINGS

Vegetable oil
2 plantains, peeled and cut into ¼-inch slices
1 teaspoon ground red chilies
2 pounds beef for stew, cut into 1-inch cubes
8 whole cloves
4 medium tomatoes, chopped (about 4 cups)
2 medium onions, each cut into fourths
2 cloves garlic, finely chopped
¼ cup chopped celery
¼ cup chopped carrot
4 cups water
2 tablespoons snipped fresh cilantro
2 teaspoons salt
1 teaspoon ground thyme
1 teaspoon ground oregano
¼ teaspoon pepper
1 cup chopped green bell pepper

Heat oil (1 inch) to 350°. Fry plantains, a few slices at a time, in oil until golden brown, about 2 minutes; drain. Toss with ground red chilies; reserve.

Heat remaining ingredients except bell pepper to boiling in 4-quart Dutch oven; reduce heat. Cover and simmer until the beef is tender, 2 to 2½ hours.

Remove beef with slotted spoon and drain. Cook broth uncovered over high heat until reduced to 3 cups. Stir in beef, plantains and bell pepper. Simmer uncovered 10 minutes.

Sauerbraten Stew

1 pound beef boneless chuck or round
    steak, cut into 1-inch pieces
1 teaspoon salt
¼ teaspoon ground cloves
¼ teaspoon pepper
1½ cups water
¼ cup red wine vinegar
1 can (10½ ounces) condensed beef broth
1 bay leaf
1 medium onion, chopped (about ½ cup)
½ small head red cabbage, coarsely
    shredded
8 gingersnaps, crushed (about ½ cup)
1 tablespoon packed brown sugar

Mix all ingredients except gingersnaps and brown sugar in 4-quart ovenproof Dutch oven. Cover and bake in 325° oven until beef is tender, about 2 hours.

Remove bay leaf. Stir gingersnaps and brown sugar into stew. Cover and bake 10 minutes. Serve with hot buttered poppy seed noodles, if desired.

TO MICROWAVE: Cut beef into ½-inch pieces. Decrease water to 1¼ cups and vinegar to 2 tablespoons. Mix all ingredients except vinegar, gingersnaps and brown sugar in 3-quart microwavable casserole. Cover tightly and microwave on high to boiling, 10 to 12 minutes; stir. Cover tightly and microwave on medium (50%), stirring every 15 minutes, until beef is tender, 35 to 45 minutes longer. Remove bay leaf.

Stir in vinegar, gingersnaps and brown sugar. Cover tightly and microwave on high until mixture thickens and boils, 3 to 4 minutes. Serve as directed above.

Beef and Tequila Stew

2 pounds beef boneless chuck, tip or
   round, cut into 1-inch cubes
1/4 cup all-purpose flour
1/4 cup vegetable oil
1 medium onion, chopped (about 1/2 cup)
2 slices bacon, cut up
1/4 cup chopped carrot
1/4 cup chopped celery
1/4 cup tequila
3/4 cup tomato juice
2 tablespoons snipped fresh cilantro
1 1/2 teaspoons salt
1 can (15 ounces) garbanzo beans
4 medium tomatoes, chopped (about
   4 cups)
2 cloves garlic, finely chopped

Coat beef with flour. Heat oil in 10-inch skillet until hot. Cook and stir beef in oil over medium heat until brown. Remove beef with slotted spoon and drain. Cook and stir onion and bacon in same skillet until bacon is crisp.

Stir in beef and remaining ingredients. Heat to boiling; reduce heat. Cover and simmer until beef is tender, about 1 hour.

Savory Pork Stew

1 pound lean pork boneless shoulder
1 large onion, chopped (about 1 cup)
1 teaspoon snipped fresh rosemary leaves
   or 1/2 teaspoon dried rosemary leaves
1 tablespoon snipped fresh basil leaves
   or 1 teaspoon dried basil leaves
1/4 teaspoon pepper
1/2 cup water
2 cups carrots, cut into 1-inch slices
   (about 6 medium)
1 large green bell pepper, cut into 1-inch
   pieces
3 cups halved mushrooms (about
   8 ounces)
1/2 cup Burgundy or other dry red wine
1 can (8 ounces) tomato sauce

Trim fat from pork shoulder; cut into 1-inch cubes. Spray 3-quart saucepan with nonstick cooking spray. Cook and stir pork over medium heat until brown. Stir in onion, rosemary, basil, pepper and water. Heat to boiling; reduce heat. Cover and simmer until pork is almost tender, about 1 hour.

Stir in remaining ingredients. Cover and simmer until vegetables are tender, stirring occasionally, about 30 minutes.

Posole

1/4 cup vegetable oil
1 clove garlic, finely chopped
1/2 pound pork boneless shoulder, cut into
   1/2-inch cubes
1/4 cup all-purpose flour
1 medium onion, chopped (about 1/2 cup)
1 can (15 ounces) pinto beans, drained
1 can (30 ounces) hominy, drained
1/4 cup chopped carrot
1/4 cup chopped celery
1/4 cup chopped green chilies
1 tablespoon ground red chilies
3 cups chicken broth
1 teaspoon salt
1/4 teaspoon pepper
1 1/2 teaspoons dried oregano leaves
1 small onion, chopped (about 1/4 cup)
1/4 cup snipped fresh cilantro
Lime wedges
Tortilla chips

Heat oil and garlic in 3-quart saucepan until oil is hot. Coat pork with flour. Cook and stir pork in oil over medium heat until brown; remove pork with slotted spoon and drain.

Cook and stir 1/2 cup onion in same saucepan until tender. Stir in beans, hominy, carrot, celery, green chilies, ground red chilies and broth. Heat to boiling; reduce heat. Cover and simmer 10 minutes.

Stir pork, salt and pepper into vegetable mixture. Heat to boiling; reduce heat. Cover and simmer 30 minutes. Sprinkle with oregano, 1/4 cup onion and the cilantro. Serve with lime wedges and tortilla chips.

Green Chili Stew

3 pounds lamb boneless shoulder
1 large onion, chopped (about 1 cup)
3 cloves garlic, finely chopped
¼ cup vegetable oil
2 cups chicken broth
1 teaspoon salt
1 teaspoon dried juniper berries, crushed
¾ teaspoon pepper
1 tablespoon all-purpose flour
¼ cup water
*4 medium poblano chilies, roasted,**
  peeled, seeded and cut into 2 × ¼-inch
  strips
2 tablespoons finely shredded lemon peel

Trim excess fat from lamb shoulder; cut lamb into 1-inch cubes. Cook and stir lamb, onion, and garlic in oil in 4-quart Dutch oven until lamb is no longer pink; drain.

Stir in broth, salt, juniper berries and pepper. Heat to boiling; reduce heat. Cover and simmer, stirring occasionally, until lamb is tender, about 1 hour.

Shake flour and water in tightly covered container; stir into lamb mixture. Heat to boiling, stirring constantly. Boil and stir 1 minute. Stir in chilies. Sprinkle each serving with lemon peel.

*To roast chilies, set oven control to broil. Arrange whole chilies with their top surfaces about 5 inches from the heat. (Some people cut a small slit in the shoulder of each chili, to prevent it from bursting.) Broil, turning occasionally, until the skin is blistered and evenly browned (*not* burned) 12 to 17 minutes. Remove chilies to a plastic bag and close tightly; let chilies sit for 20 minutes, then peel. Anaheim and poblano chilies will roast in 12 to 17 minutes, jalapeño and serrano chilies, in about 5 minutes.

Following pages: Green Chili Stew, left, and Easy Burgundy Stew, right (page 61)

Pork Stew with Corn Bread Topping

8 SERVINGS

1 small red bell pepper
1 small yellow bell pepper
1 pound pork boneless loin, cut into
    1-inch cubes
1/2 pound bulk chorizo sausage
1 large onion, chopped (about 1 cup)
2 cloves garlic, finely chopped
1 cup beef broth
1 tablespoon dried basil leaves
1 tablespoon dried cilantro leaves
2 teaspoons ground red chilies
1 cup whole kernel corn
1 medium tomato, chopped (about 1 cup)
1 small butternut or acorn squash, pared
    and cut into 1/2-inch cubes (about 1
    cup)
1 can (2 1/4 ounces) sliced ripe olives,
    drained (about 1/2 cup)
Corn Bread Topping (below)
Salsa

Cut 5 thin slices from each bell pepper; reserve slices. Chop remaining bell peppers (about 1/2 cup each). Cook pork, sausage, onion and garlic in 4-quart Dutch oven over medium heat, stirring occasionally, until pork is no longer pink; drain. Stir in chopped bell peppers, broth, basil, cilantro and ground red chilies. Heat to boiling; reduce heat. Cover and simmer 30 minutes, stirring occasionally. Stir corn, tomato, squash and olives into meat mixture; cook 15 minutes longer.

Heat oven to 425°. Prepare Corn Bread Topping. Pour meat mixture into ungreased rectangular baking dish, 13 × 9 × 2 inches, or 3-quart shallow casserole. Pour Corn Bread Topping over meat mixture; carefully spread to cover, sealing to edge of dish. Arrange reserved bell pepper slices on top. Bake until topping is golden brown, 15 to 20 minutes. Serve with salsa.

CORN BREAD TOPPING

1 1/2 cups yellow cornmeal
1/2 cup all-purpose flour
1 cup dairy sour cream
2/3 cup milk
1/4 cup vegetable oil
2 teaspoons baking powder
1/2 teaspoon baking soda
1/2 teaspoon salt
1 egg

Mix all ingredients; beat vigorously 30 seconds.

Irish Lamb Stew

2 pounds lamb boneless neck or shoulder,
cut into 1-inch pieces
6 medium potatoes, cut into ½-inch slices
(about 2 pounds)
3 medium onions, sliced
2 teaspoons salt
¼ teaspoon pepper
2 cups water
Snipped parsley

Layer half each of the lamb, potatoes and onions in 4-quart Dutch oven; sprinkle with half each of the salt and pepper. Repeat; add water.

Heat to boiling; reduce heat. Cover and simmer until lamb is tender, 1½ to 2 hours. Skim fat from broth (see note). Sprinkle stew with parsley. Serve in bowls with pickled red cabbage, if desired.

TO MICROWAVE: Cut lamb into ½-inch pieces. Cut potatoes into ¼-inch slices. Omit water. Place lamb in 3-quart microwavable casserole. Cover tightly and microwave on high 6 minutes; stir. Cover tightly and microwave until very little pink remains, 6 to 9 minutes longer. Drain, reserving ½ cup drippings.

Arrange potatoes in square microwavable dish, 8 × 8 × 2 inches; sprinkle with 2 tablespoons water. Cover tightly and microwave on high until barely tender, 8 to 12 minutes.

Add potatoes, onions, salt and pepper to lamb in 3-quart casserole; stir. Pour reserved drippings over top. Cover tightly and microwave on medium-low (30%) 20 minutes; stir. Cover tightly and microwave until lamb is tender, 20 to 28 minutes longer. Continue as directed above.

Note: To remove fat easily, prepare stew the day before, cover and refrigerate. Remove fat before reheating.

Lamb and Barley Stew

2 pounds lamb boneless shoulder, cut into
  1-inch pieces
1 teaspoon salt
2 teaspoons snipped fresh rosemary leaves
  or ³/₄ teaspoon dried rosemary leaves,
  crushed
¹/₄ teaspoon pepper
2 cloves garlic, finely chopped
¹/₂ cup uncooked barley
1 medium onion, chopped (about ¹/₂ cup)
4 medium carrots, cut into 1-inch pieces
2 cups water

Place lamb in 4-quart Dutch oven. Sprinkle with salt, rosemary, pepper and garlic.

Layer barley, onion and carrots on top. Pour water over carrots. Cover and bake in 325° oven until lamb and barley are tender, about 2 hours.

TO MICROWAVE: Cut lamb into ¹/₂-inch pieces and carrots into ¹/₂-inch slices. Decrease water to 1³/₄ cups and use hot water.

Place lamb in 3-quart microwavable casserole. Cover tightly and microwave on high 6 minutes; stir. Cover tightly and microwave until no longer pink, 6 to 8 minutes longer (do not drain).

Stir in remaining ingredients. Cover tightly and microwave to boiling, 8 to 10 minutes; stir. Cover tightly and microwave on medium-low (30%), stirring every 15 minutes, until barley is tender, 40 to 50 minutes longer.

· 5 ·

DIFFERENT DINNERS

Braised Beef Esterhazy

1½ pounds beef boneless round steak,
  ½ inch thick
3 tablespoons all-purpose flour
2 tablespoons vegetable oil
1 can (10½ ounces) condensed beef broth
½ cup water
3 carrots, cut into strips, 3 × ½ inch
3 medium parsnips, cut into strips,
  3 × ½ inch
2 medium onions, sliced
1 teaspoon salt
¼ teaspoon pepper
¼ teaspoon dried thyme leaves
3 sweet gherkin pickles, cut lengthwise
  into ¼-inch strips
1 cup dairy sour cream

Sprinkle one side of beef with half the flour; pound in. Turn beef; pound in remaining flour. Cut into 6 serving pieces. Heat oil in 12-inch skillet until hot. Cook 3 or 4 pieces of beef at a time in oil over medium heat until brown on both sides, about 15 minutes; drain.

Add beef broth and water. Heat to boiling; reduce heat. Cover and simmer 15 minutes. Add carrots, parsnips and onions. Sprinkle with salt, pepper and thyme. Cover and simmer until beef and vegetables are tender, 40 to 60 minutes. Add gherkins during last 5 minutes.

Remove beef and vegetables to heated platter. Skim fat from broth if necessary; stir in sour cream. Heat just until hot. Serve gravy with beef and vegetables.

Stuffed Rolled Steak

8 SERVINGS

*1½ pound beef boneless round steak,
   ½ inch thick*
1½ teaspoons salt
½ teaspoon dried oregano leaves
¼ teaspoon pepper
*4 ounces thinly sliced fully cooked smoked
   ham*
2 medium tomatoes, chopped
*1 can (4 ounces) mild green chilies,
   drained and chopped*
1 medium onion, chopped (about ½ cup)
1 clove garlic, finely chopped
¼ cup dry bread crumbs
1 medium carrot
*1 hard-cooked egg, peeled and cut
   lengthwise into fourths*
½ teaspoon salt
2 tablespoons vegetable oil
¾ cup water
1 teaspoon vinegar
1 teaspoon Worcestershire sauce
1 bay leaf

Trim fat from beef. Pound until ¼ inch thick. Sprinkle beef with 1½ teaspoons salt, the oregano and pepper. Arrange ham evenly on beef. Sprinkle tomatoes, chilies, onion, garlic and bread crumbs on ham.

Cut carrot lengthwise into halves; cut halves lengthwise into 3 strips. Arrange on ham. Place egg pieces down center of ham. Sprinkle with ½ teaspoon salt. Carefully roll up beef. Fasten with metal skewers or tie with string. (If beef separates when rolled, fasten with wooden picks.)

Heat oil in Dutch oven until hot. Carefully transfer beef roll to Dutch oven; cook over medium heat until brown on all sides. Drain fat. Add water, vinegar, Worcestershire sauce and bay leaf. Cover and cook in 325° oven until beef is tender, about 1½ hours. Remove skewers. Cut beef. Remove bay leaf from cooking liquid; serve beef with cooking liquid.

Herbed Cube Steak in Foil

4 SERVINGS

4 beef cubed steaks
1 can (16 ounces) whole kernel corn
1 medium tomato, cut into 8 slices
1 medium onion, cut into 8 slices
*4 ounces small fresh mushrooms (about
   1 cup)*
½ cup margarine or butter
*3 tablespoons snipped fresh herb leaves,
   if desired*
Salt and pepper to taste

Place each beef cubed steak on piece of heavy-duty aluminum foil. Place ½ cup of corn and 2 slices each of tomato and onion on side of each steak; place mushrooms on top. Top steaks and mushrooms with 2 tablespoons margarine each. Sprinkle with herbs, salt and pepper.

Wrap securely in foil. Place packets on cooking grill or on coals. Cook, turning once, until done, 35 to 40 minutes on grill, 15 to 20 minutes on coals.

Cornish Pasties

1 pound beef top round or chuck steak
Pastry (below)
2 medium onions, chopped (about 1 cup)
2 cups cubed potatoes (2 large)
1 cup diced rutabaga or carrots
2 teaspoons salt
1/4 teaspoon pepper
Margarine or butter
Water
Milk or half-and-half
Hot mustard

Cut beef into 1/2-inch pieces. (For ease in cutting, partially freeze beef about 1 hour.) Prepare Pastry; divide into 6 equal parts. Roll each part into 9-inch circle. Place on two ungreased cookie sheets. Toss beef, onions, potatoes, rutabaga, salt and pepper. Heat oven to 375°.

Place about 1 cup filling on half of each circle. Dot each with about 1 teaspoon margarine and sprinkle with about 2 teaspoons water. Moisten edge of each circle with water; fold over. Press edges with fork to seal. Cut slits or design in top of each; brush with milk. Bake until crust is golden brown, 50 to 55 minutes. Serve hot or cold with hot mustard.

PASTRY

1 cup plus 2 tablespoons shortening
3 cups all-purpose flour
1 1/2 teaspoons salt
5 to 6 tablespoons cold water

Cut shortening into flour and salt until particles are size of small peas. Sprinkle in water, 1 tablespoon at a time, tossing with fork until all flour is moistened and pastry almost cleans side of bowl (1 to 2 teaspoons water can be added if necessary). Gather pastry into a ball.

Following pages: Cornish Pasties

Spinach Manicotti

7 SERVINGS

1 pound ground beef
1 large onion, chopped (about 1 cup)
2 large cloves garlic, crushed
1 can (28 ounces) whole tomatoes
1 can (8 ounces) mushroom stems and
    pieces, drained
1/4 cup snipped parsley
1 teaspoon salt
1 teaspoon fennel seed
1 teaspoon dried basil leaves
2 packages (10 ounces each) frozen
    chopped spinach
2 cups creamed cottage cheese (small
    curd)
1/3 cup grated Parmesan cheese
1/4 teaspoon ground nutmeg
1/4 teaspoon pepper
14 uncooked manicotti shells
2 tablespoons grated Parmesan cheese

Cook and stir ground beef, onion and garlic in 10-inch skillet until beef is brown, about 10 minutes; drain. Stir in tomatoes (with liquid), mushrooms, parsley, salt, fennel seed and basil; break up tomatoes. Heat to boiling; reduce heat. Cover and simmer beef mixture 10 minutes.

Spoon about 1/3 of the beef mixture in ungreased rectangular baking dish, 13 × 9 × 2 inches. Rinse spinach under running cold water to separate; drain. Place spinach on towels and squeeze until dry. Mix spinach, cottage cheese, 1/3 cup Parmesan cheese, the nutmeg and pepper. Fill uncooked manicotti shells with spinach mixture; place shells on beef mixture in dish. Pour remaining beef mixture evenly over shells, covering shells completely; sprinkle with 2 tablespoons Parmesan cheese. Cover and cook in 350° oven until shells are tender, about 1½ hours.

Layered Beef

6 SERVINGS

1½ pounds ground beef
1 medium onion, chopped (about 1/2 cup)
1 egg
1/2 cup milk
1/3 cup dry bread crumbs
1 teaspoon salt
1 teaspoon dried basil leaves
1/4 teaspoon garlic powder
1/2 cup shredded Swiss cheese (about
    2 ounces)
2 small zucchini, thinly sliced (about
    1 1/3 cups)
1 jar (2 ounces) diced pimiento, drained

Mix ground beef, onion, egg, milk, bread crumbs, salt, basil and garlic powder. Spread half of the beef mixture in ungreased square pan, 8 × 8 × 2 inches. Sprinkle cheese, zucchini and pimiento over beef mixture to within 1/2 inch of sides of pan; spread remaining beef mixture carefully over top. Cook uncovered in 350° oven until done, 45 to 50 minutes; drain off fat. Let stand 10 minutes before cutting into serving pieces.

Chinese Hot Pot

1/2 pound pork tenderloin, top sirloin of beef or boneless lamb

1 whole chicken breast, skinned and boned, or 1/2 pound chicken livers, cut into halves

1/2 pound cleaned raw shrimp, cut lengthwise into halves, or 1/2 pound scallops, cut into 3/4-inch pieces

8 ounces bean curd, cut into 1/2-inch cubes

8 ounces broccoli, separated into flowerets and sliced

1 package (6 ounces) frozen Chinese pea pods or 4 ounces spinach, stems trimmed

8 ounces mushrooms, sliced

1/4 head cauliflower, separated into flowerets and sliced

2 medium carrots, cut diagonally into 1/8-inch slices

1 bunch green onions (about 8), trimmed and cut into 1 1/2-inch pieces

3 ounces cellophane noodles

3 cups warm water

8 cups chicken broth

Dipping Sauces (Soy sauce, teriyaki sauce, Chinese plum sauce, hoisin sauce or mustard sauce)

Choose 2 meats or combination of meat and seafood and 3 vegetables from selections at left. Cut pork, beef or lamb across grain into 1/8-inch slices; cut chicken breast across grain into 1/4-inch slices. (For ease in cutting, partially freeze meat or chicken breast about 1 hour.) Divide meat, seafood and vegetables among serving trays or plates; arrange attractively in overlapping layers. Garnish each with parsley, if desired. Cover and refrigerate until serving time.

Place cellophane noodles in oblong baking dish; cover with water. Let stand 30 minutes. Drain; cut noodles into 6-inch pieces.

Pour chicken broth into 12-inch electric skillet until half full; heat to boiling. Pass trays of meat, seafood and vegetables. Guests choose an assortment and, with chopsticks or fondue forks, place the food in hot broth to cook until done, 1 to 4 minutes. (Add hot chicken broth as needed.) Serve with 2 or 3 Dipping Sauces.

When the meat and seafood have been eaten, place the cellophane noodles and any remaining vegetables in remaining broth in the skillet. Cook until tender, 1 to 2 minutes. Ladle noodles and broth into soup bowls; serve as the last course.

Following pages: Chinese Hot Pot

Beef and Corn Pie

1 pound ground beef
1 medium onion, chopped (about 1/2 cup)
1 can (8 3/4 ounces) whole kernel corn, drained
1 can (8 ounces) tomato sauce
1 small green pepper, chopped (about 1/2 cup)
1 teaspoon dried basil leaves
1/2 teaspoon salt
1/2 teaspoon dried oregano leaves
1/4 teaspoon red pepper sauce
Cornmeal Crust (below)
1/2 cup shredded Cheddar cheese (about 2 ounces)

Cook and stir ground beef and onion in 10-inch skillet until beef is brown, about 10 minutes; drain. Stir in corn, tomato sauce, green pepper, basil, salt, oregano and pepper sauce. Prepare Cornmeal Crust. Press firmly and evenly against bottom and side of ungreased pie plate, 9 × 1 1/4 inches. Spoon beef mixture into pie plate. Cook uncovered in 400° oven 25 minutes. Sprinkle cheese over beef mixture. Cook until cheese is melted, about 5 minutes longer. Let stand 10 minutes before cutting.

CORNMEAL CRUST

1 cup all-purpose flour
1/4 cup yellow cornmeal
1/4 teaspoon salt
1/3 cup margarine or butter, softened
3 to 4 tablespoons water

Mix flour, cornmeal and salt. Stir in margarine and enough water to make a soft dough.

Sweet-Sour Cabbage Rolls

8 large cabbage leaves
1 pound ground beef
1/3 cup uncooked bulgur
1/3 cup milk
1 egg
1 teaspoon salt
1 teaspoon dry mustard
1/4 teaspoon pepper
1/4 teaspoon ground cinnamon
1/2 cup packed brown sugar
1/2 cup water
1/4 cup vinegar
1 teaspoon caraway seed
4 medium potatoes, cut into fourths
1 tablespoon cornstarch
2 tablespoons cold water

Cover cabbage leaves with boiling water. Let stand until leaves are limp, about 10 minutes; drain. Mix ground beef, bulgur, milk, egg, salt, mustard, pepper and cinnamon. Shape beef mixture into eight 3½-inch rolls. Place 1 roll across stem end of each cabbage leaf. Roll leaf around roll, folding in sides. Place rolls seam sides down in Dutch oven.

Mix brown sugar, ½ cup water, the vinegar and caraway seed; pour over rolls. Heat to boiling; reduce heat. Cover and simmer 30 minutes. Add potatoes. Cover and simmer until potatoes are tender, about 30 minutes. Remove rolls and potatoes; keep warm. Mix cornstarch and 2 tablespoons cold water; gradually stir into broth. Heat to boiling, stirring constantly. Boil and stir 1 minute.

TO MICROWAVE: Prepare cabbage rolls as directed. Arrange in circle in 3-quart round microwavable casserole. Mix brown sugar, ½ cup water, the vinegar and caraway seed; pour over cabbage rolls. Add potatoes around edge of casserole. Cover tightly and microwave on high 10 minutes; rotate casserole ½ turn. Microwave until cabbage rolls are done and potatoes are tender, 10 to 15 minutes longer. Remove cabbage rolls and potatoes; keep warm. Mix cornstarch and 2 tablespoons cold water; gradually stir into broth. Microwave uncovered, stirring every minute until thickened, 3 to 4 minutes. Serve with rolls.

Pork Florentine

³/₄ pound lean pork tenderloin, cut into
  6 slices
2 teaspoons margarine or butter
2 teaspoons olive or vegetable oil
Swiss Cheese Sauce (below)
1 medium onion, chopped (about ¹/₂ cup)
1 clove garlic, finely chopped
1 tablespoon margarine or butter
¹/₂ teaspoon salt
¹/₄ teaspoon pepper
¹/₄ teaspoon ground nutmeg
1 pound fresh spinach
1 tablespoon lemon juice
Ground nutmeg

Pound pork tenderloin slices until ¹/₄ inch thick. Heat 1 teaspoon of the margarine and 1 teaspoon of the oil in 4-quart Dutch oven over medium-low heat until hot. Cook 3 slices pork in oil mixture, turning once, until done, about 10 minutes. Remove pork from skillet; keep warm. Repeat with remaining margarine, oil and pork.

Prepare Swiss Cheese Sauce. Cook and stir onion and garlic in 1 tablespoon margarine in 4-quart Dutch oven over medium heat until onion is tender, about 3 minutes. Stir in salt, pepper and nutmeg. Add spinach; toss just until spinach is wilted. Drizzle with lemon juice. Arrange spinach on serving platter; place pork over spinach. Serve with Swiss Cheese Sauce. Sprinkle with nutmeg.

SWISS CHEESE SAUCE

1 tablespoon cornstarch
³/₄ cup milk
2 tablespoons plain yogurt
¹/₂ cup shredded Swiss cheese (2 ounces)
¹/₄ teaspoon ground nutmeg

Mix cornstarch and milk. Cook over medium heat until mixture thickens and boils, stirring constantly. Boil and stir 1 minute; remove from heat. Stir in cheese and nutmeg; heat until cheese melts.

Pork with Apple and Parsnips

4 pork loin or rib chops, about ½ inch
   thick
3 medium parsnips, cut crosswise into
   ½-inch slices
1 medium onion, sliced
½ cup chicken broth
1 teaspoon dry mustard
½ teaspoon salt
¼ teaspoon ground allspice
⅛ teaspoon pepper
1 medium apple, cut into ¼-inch wedges
2 tablespoons snipped parsley

Cook pork in 10-inch skillet over medium heat until brown on both sides. Place parsnips and onion on pork. Mix chicken broth, mustard, salt, allspice and pepper; pour over vegetables. Heat to boiling; reduce heat. Cover and simmer until pork is done, 35 to 40 minutes. Arrange apple on vegetables. Cover and cook just until apple is tender, about 3 minutes. Sprinkle with parsley.

Autumn Pork Chops

6 pork loin or rib chops, about ½ inch
   thick
¼ teaspoon salt
⅛ teaspoon pepper
2 medium onions, sliced and separated
   into rings
2 medium acorn squash, cut into 1-inch
   rings and seeded
3 medium apples, cored and cut into
   1-inch rings
¼ cup margarine or butter, melted
2 tablespoons honey
2 tablespoons water
1 teaspoon pumpkin pie spice

Cook pork over medium heat until brown on both sides. Place pork in ungreased rectangular baking dish, 13 × 9 × 2 inches; sprinkle with salt and pepper. Arrange onions, squash and apples on pork. Mix remaining ingredients; pour over apples. Cover and cook in 350° oven until pork is done and squash is tender, 45 to 55 minutes. Serve pan drippings with pork.

Following pages: Autumn Pork Chops, left, and Spareribs and Cabbage, right (page 92)

Pork and Broccoli Risotto

6 SERVINGS

1 pound lean pork boneless loin or leg
2 teaspoons vegetable oil
3 cups broccoli flowerets
1 cup chopped red bell pepper
2 cloves garlic, finely chopped
1 teaspoon salt
1 medium onion, chopped (about 1/2 cup)
1 tablespoon margarine or butter
1 cup uncooked long grain or Arborio
   rice
1/4 cup dry white wine
1 cup beef broth
1 1/4 cups water
1/4 cup milk
2 tablespoons grated Parmesan cheese

Trim fat from pork loin; cut pork into slices, 2 × 1 × 1/4 inch. Heat vegetable oil in 10-inch skillet over medium heat. Cook and stir pork, broccoli, bell pepper, garlic and salt in oil until pork is done and vegetables are crisp-tender, about 5 minutes. Remove from skillet; keep warm.

In same skillet, cook onion in margarine until onion is tender, about 3 minutes. Stir in rice and wine; cook and stir until wine is absorbed, about 30 seconds. Stir in broth and water; heat to boiling. Reduce heat; cover and cook until rice is almost tender and mixture is creamy, about 15 minutes. Stir in milk and reserved pork mixture; heat through. Sprinkle with Parmesan cheese.

Spareribs and Cabbage

6 SERVINGS

1 tablespoon vegetable oil
4 1/2 pounds fresh pork spareribs, cut into
   6 pieces
1 large onion, sliced
1 large carrot, sliced
2 teaspoons instant beef bouillon
1/2 teaspoon salt
1/2 teaspoon caraway seed
1/4 teaspoon coarsely ground pepper
1 bay leaf
2 cups water
1/2 cup vinegar
1 small head green cabbage, cut into
   6 wedges
Freshly ground pepper

Heat oil in Dutch oven until hot. Cook pork spareribs, a few pieces at a time, over medium heat until brown on all sides, about 15 minutes; drain fat. Add onion, carrot, bouillon (dry), salt, caraway seed, 1/4 teaspoon pepper and the bay leaf. Pour water and vinegar over pork mixture. Heat to boiling; reduce heat. Cover and simmer 1 1/2 hours.

Add cabbage; sprinkle with pepper. Cover and simmer until cabbage is tender, about 45 minutes. Remove bay leaf. Arrange spareribs and vegetables on serving platter. Garnish with snipped parsley, if desired.

Grilled Italian Sausage Kabobs

6 SERVINGS

½ cup pizza sauce
1 tablespoon dried basil leaves
1 tablespoon vegetable oil
1½ pounds Italian-style sausage links, cut into 1½-inch pieces
2 medium-zucchini, cut into 1-inch pieces
1 medium red pepper, cut into 1½-inch pieces
1 medium green pepper, cut into 1½-inch pieces
6 large pimiento-stuffed olives

Mix pizza sauce, basil and oil; reserve. Cook sausage pieces over medium heat until partially cooked, about 10 minutes; drain. Alternate sausage pieces, zucchini pieces and pepper pieces on each of 6 metal skewers, leaving space between foods. Place olive on tip of each skewer.

Cover and grill kabobs 5 to 6 inches from medium coals, turning and brushing 2 or 3 times with pizza sauce mixture, until sausage is done and vegetables are crisp-tender, 20 to 25 minutes.

TO BROIL: Set oven control to broil. Broil sausage pieces until partially cooked; prepare sauce and kabobs as directed above. Place kabobs on rack in broiler pan. Broil with tops about 5 inches from heat, turning and brushing 2 or 3 times with pizza sauce mixture, until sausage is done and vegetables are tender, about 15 minutes.

Following pages: Lamb Shish Kabob (page 96)

Lamb Shish Kabob

1 pound lamb boneless shoulder, cut into
   1-inch cubes
1/4 cup lemon juice
2 tablespoons olive or vegetable oil
2 teaspoons salt
1/2 teaspoon dried oregano leaves
1/4 teaspoon pepper
1 medium green pepper, cut into 1-inch
   pieces
1 medium onion, cut into eighths
1 cup cubed eggplant

Place lamb in glass or plastic bowl. Mix lemon juice, oil, salt, oregano and pepper; pour over lamb. Cover and refrigerate, stirring occasionally, at least 6 hours.

Remove lamb; reserve marinade. Thread lamb on four 11-inch metal skewers, leaving a space between each piece of meat. Set oven control to broil or 550°. Broil lamb with tops about 3 inches from heat 5 minutes. Turn; brush with reserved marinade. Broil 5 minutes longer.

Alternate green pepper, onion and eggplant on four 11-inch metal skewers, leaving space between vegetables. Place vegetables on rack in broiler pan with lamb. Turn lamb again; brush lamb and vegetables with reserved marinade. Broil kabobs, turning and brushing twice with marinade, until brown, 4 to 5 minutes.

RED SPOON TIPS

Types of Meat

Selecting meat can be confusing without solid guidelines to follow. The chart following will show you how to identify specific cuts of meat by the type of bone in the cut, give you the meat's common name and explain how the meat should best be cooked.

HOW TO IDENTIFY CUTS OF MEAT BY THE BONES

TYPE OF BONE	COMMON NAME	GENERAL COOKING METHOD
Arm		
	beef chuck arm steak	braise, cook in liquid
	beef chuck arm pot roast	braise, cook in liquid
	lamb shoulder arm chop	braise, broil, panfry
	lamb shoulder arm roast	roast
	pork shoulder arm steak	braise, panfry
	pork shoulder arm roast	roast
	veal shoulder arm steak	braise, panfry
	veal shoulder arm roast	braise, roast
Blade center cuts		
	beef chuck blade steak	braise, cook in liquid
	beef chuck blade pot roast	braise, cook in liquid
	lamb shoulder blade chop	braise, broil, panfry
	lamb shoulder blade roast	roast
	pork shoulder blade steak	braise, broil, panfry
	pork shoulder blade Boston roast	braise, roast

(cont.)

97

TYPE OF BONE	COMMON NAME	GENERAL COOKING METHOD
	veal shoulder blade steak	braise, panfry
	veal shoulder blade roast	braise, roast
Rib		
backbone and rib bone	beef rib steak	broil, panfry
	beef rib roast	roast
	lamb rib chop	broil, panfry
	lamb rib roast	roast
	pork rib chop	braise, broil, panfry
	pork rib roast	roast
	veal rib chop	braise, panfry
	veal rib roast	roast
Loin		
backbone (T-shape)	beef loin steak (T-bone, porterhouse)	broil, panfry
	beef loin tenderloin roast or steak	roast, broil
	lamb loin chop	broil, panfry
	lamb loin roast	roast
	pork loin chop	braise, broil, panfry
	pork loin roast	roast
	veal loin chop	braise, panfry
	veal loin roast	roast, braise
Hip		
pin bone (near short loin)	beef sirloin steak	broil, panfry
	beef loin tenderloin roast or steak	roast, broil
flat bone (center cuts)	lamb sirloin chop	broil, panfry
	lamb leg roast	roast
	pork sirloin chop	braise, broil, panfry
	pork sirloin roast	roast
wedge bone (near round)	veal sirloin steak	braise, panfry
	veal leg sirloin roast	roast

TYPE OF BONE	COMMON NAME	GENERAL COOKING METHOD
Leg leg or round bone	beef round steak	braise, panfry
	beef rump roast	braise, roast
	lamb leg steak	broil, panfry
	lamb leg roast	roast
	pork leg (ham) steak	braise, broil, panfry
	pork leg roast (fresh or smoked)	roast
	veal leg round steak	braise, panfry
	veal leg roast	braise, roast
Breast breast and rib	beef brisket (fresh or corned)	braise, cook in liquid
	beef plate short rib	braise, cook in liquid
	lamb breast	roast, braise
	lamb breast riblet	braise, cook in liquid
	pork bacon (side pork)	broil, panfry, bake
	pork sparerib	roast, braise, cook in liquid
	veal breast	roast, braise
	veal breast riblet	braise, cook in liquid

The Perfect Roast

A well-cooked roast always makes a delicious meal, whether it's beef, veal, lamb or pork. It is important to be sure that a roast has been properly cooked, and by following these tips, as well as the timetables given below and on the next page, you will always have a perfect roast.

BEEF AND VEAL

- Allow roughly ⅓ pound uncooked per person. Allow less for boneless roasts, more for roasts with a bone.

- Place beef or veal, fat side up, on a rack in a shallow roasting pan. With a rib roast, the ribs will form a natural rack.

- If a veal roast has little or no fat, place 2 or 3 slices of bacon or salt pork on top of the roast to keep it from drying out.

- Insert meat thermometer so that the tip is in the center of the thickest part of the beef or veal and does not touch bone or rest in fat.

- Do not add water to the roast and do not cover.

- Roast in a 325° oven to desired doneness—see timetable below.

- Roasts that sit for 15 to 20 minutes after they are removed from the oven are easier to carve. Meat continues to cook after removal from the oven, so take out the roast when meat thermometer registers 5° to 10° lower than desired doneness.

LAMB

- Allow about ⅓ pound uncooked lamb per person. Allow less for boneless roasts, more for roasts with a bone.

- Follow beef guideline for cooking preparations and for resting time before carving.

PORK

- Allow about ⅓ pound uncooked per person. Allow less for boneless roasts, more for roasts with a bone.

- Fresh hams should be cooked to 170°. A ham labeled "Cook before eating" should be cooked to 160°.

- Follow beef guidelines for cooking preparations and for resting time before carving.

- See timetable on page 103 for roasting times for uncooked hams.

TIMETABLE FOR ROASTING BEEF (OVEN TEMPERATURE 325°F)

CUT	APPROXIMATE WEIGHT (POUNDS)	MEAT THERMOMETER READING (°F)	APPROXIMATE COOKING TIME (MINUTES PER POUND)
Rib	6 to 8	140° (rare)	23 to 25
		160° (medium)	27 to 30
		170° (well)	32 to 35
Boneless Rib	4 to 6	140° (rare)	26 to 32
		160° (medium)	34 to 38
		170° (well)	40 to 42
Rib Eye (Delmonico)*	4 to 6	140° (rare)	18 to 20
		160° (medium)	20 to 22
		170° (well)	22 to 24
Rolled Rump (high quality)	4 to 6	150° to 170°	25 to 30
Tip (high quality)	3½ to 4	140° to 170°	35 to 40
	6 to 8	140° to 170°	30 to 35
Top Round (high quality)	4 to 6	140° to 170°	25 to 30

CUT	APPROXIMATE WEIGHT (POUNDS)	MEAT THERMOMETER READING (°F)	APPROXIMATE COOKING TIME (MINUTES PER POUND)
			TOTAL COOKING TIME
Tenderloin (whole)	4 to 6	140° (rare)	45 to 60 minutes
Tenderloin (half)	2 to 3	140° (rare)	45 to 50 minutes

*Roast at 350° **Roast at 425°

TIMETABLE FOR ROASTING VEAL
(OVEN TEMPERATURE 325°F)

CUT	APPROXIMATE WEIGHT (POUNDS)	APPROXIMATE COOKING TIME* (MINUTES PER POUND)
Round or Sirloin	5 to 8	25 to 35
Loin	4 to 6	30 to 35
Rib	3 to 5	35 to 40
Boneless Rump	3 to 5	40 to 45
Boneless Shoulder	4 to 6	40 to 45

*Meat thermometer reading 170°F

TIMETABLE FOR ROASTING LAMB
(OVEN TEMPERATURE 325°F)

CUT	APPROXIMATE WEIGHT (POUNDS)	MEAT THERMOMETER READING (°F)	APPROXIMATE COOKING TIME (MINUTES PER POUND)
Leg	7 to 9	140° (rare)	15 to 20
		160° (medium)	20 to 25
		170° (well)	25 to 30
Leg	5 to 7	140° (rare)	20 to 25
		160° (medium)	25 to 30
		170° (well)	30 to 35
Leg, Boneless	4 to 7	140° (rare)	25 to 30
		160° (medium)	30 to 35
		170° (well)	35 to 40
Leg, Shank Half	3 to 4	140° (rare)	30 to 35
		160° (medium)	40 to 45
		170° (well)	45 to 50
Leg, Sirloin Half	3 to 4	140° (rare)	25 to 30
		160° (medium)	35 to 40
		170° (well)	45 to 50
Shoulder, Boneless	3½ to 5	140° (rare)	30 to 35
		160° (medium)	35 to 40
		170° (well)	40 to 45

TIMETABLE FOR ROASTING FRESH PORK
(OVEN TEMPERATURE 325°F)

CUT	APPROXIMATE WEIGHT (POUNDS)	MEAT THERMOMETER READING (°F)	APPROXIMATE COOKING TIME (MINUTES PER POUND)
Fresh Loin			
Center	3 to 5	170°	30 to 35
Half	5 to 7	170°	35 to 40
Blade or Sirloin	3 to 4	170°	40 to 45
Boneless Top (double)	3 to 5	170°	35 to 45
Boneless Top	2 to 4	170°	30 to 35

CUT	APPROXIMATE WEIGHT (POUNDS)	MEAT THERMOMETER READING (°F)	APPROXIMATE COOKING TIME (MINUTES PER POUND)
Fresh Arm Picnic	5 to 8	170°	30 to 35
Fresh Boston Shoulder			
Boneless Blade Boston	3 to 5	170°	35 to 40
Blade Boston	4 to 6	170°	40 to 45
Fresh Leg (Ham)			
Whole (bone-in)	12 to 14	170°	22 to 26
Boneless	10 to 14	170°	24 to 28
Half (bone-in)	5 to 8	170°	35 to 40
			TOTAL COOKING TIME
Fresh Tenderloin	½ to 1	170°	¾ to 1 hour
Fresh Spareribs, Back Ribs and Country-style Ribs		Cooked well done	1½ to 2½ hours

Microwaving Roasts

Microwaving lets you have a roast in a hurry, without sacrificing flavor. Follow these guidelines for a tip-top roast.

BEEF ROASTS

▪ Choose a high-quality roast with a uniform shape. Some good choices are boneless top round, sirloin tip, rump or rib eye roast (small end).

▪ Tenderize less tender roasts with a marinade or commercial tenderizer.

▪ Place roast on a microwavable rack high enough to keep meat above its juices. Do not add water.

▪ Cover loosely (if directed) so that the meat will not be steamed.

▪ Use low (30%) or medium (50%) power to prevent shrinkage and retain juiciness, tenderness, flavor and appearance.

▪ Use brush-on sauces or browning shake-ons to enhance color and add flavor.

▪ Start cooking with fat side down. Turn roast over after about half the cooking time.

▪ Use a microwave thermometer or temperature probe inserted horizontally during cooking, or insert a conventional meat thermometer after cooking. (Adjust cooking time to allow for internal temperature of meat to rise during standing time.)

- Add a standing time of 10 to 20 minutes with meat covered with aluminum foil to even the cooking. (Allow for internal temperature to rise as meat stands.)

Microwaving Pork

- All pork, except fully cooked smoked pork, must be cooked until well done. A meat thermometer should register 170° throughout the meat. When microwaving a pork roast or chops, check several places in the meat with a meat thermometer and cook longer if necessary. Check several chops for doneness, not just one.

- Never substitute uncooked pork when a recipe calls for cooked pork, such as ham, Polish sausage and cooked luncheon meat. The time given in the recipe will not be sufficient to cook the meat safely.

Microwaving Meat and Gravy

Thinly slice meat, or cut it into uniform pieces. Top with gravy or other sauce, such as a barbecue sauce, and cover loosely.

From Tough to Tender

The most tender cuts of meat are the most expensive, but less expensive cuts can be tenderized with an artful marinade, and an everyday cut can turn into company best. The marinade suggestions following are your guide to tasty, tender results.

- Don't marinate meat longer than 24 hours.

- Marinate meat in a glass container be-cause it can withstand the acid in the marinade. Earthenware and metals other than stainless steel are not recommended because they react with acid.

- Always store meat that is marinating in the refrigerator, not at room temperature.

Marinades

FRESH LEMON JUICE: Combine with oil and herbs.

SOY SAUCE: Combine with honey, garlic, herbs—or use alone.

TOMATO JUICE OR SAUCE: Combine with soy sauce, garlic, oil and seasonings. This is particularly good on very tough meat.

VINEGAR: Combine with oil and herbs to make a vinaigrette. If you're pressed for time, try bottled vinaigrette.

WINE: In general, red wine is used, and combined with oil, spices and garlic.

After the meat has marinated, grill, broil or roast.

Varied Vegetables

Vegetables have become even more popular recently due to the increased variety found in supermarkets, the recognition of their importance to a healthful diet and the almost year-round availability of vegetables that used to be seasonal. Even those who might have needed coaxing are learning that vegetables are a delight with their fresh flavors and vibrant colors, whether eaten raw in salads or crudités, or properly cooked and seasoned. Many people don't realize how easy it is to select succulent fresh vegetables, or to cook their vegetables once they bring them home. The following suggestions will help you select the best vegetables, and learn the easiest way to cook them.

Beans (String, Stringless)

Select long, crisp pods with fresh-looking tips and bright green or waxy yellow color. Beans may be flat, long and round or have a velvety pod, depending on variety.

Wash beans and remove ends. Leave beans whole or cut French style into lengthwise strips or crosswise into 1-inch pieces.

Broccoli

Choose firm, compact, dark green or purplish green clusters of small flower buds, with none sufficiently open to show yellow flowers. Stalks should be tender, firm and not too thick.

Trim off large leaves; remove tough ends of lower stems and wash broccoli. Trim into portion size before cooking.

Tip: If broccoli stems are more than 1 inch thick, make lengthwise gash for even cooking.

Cabbage (Green, Savoy and Red)

Look for well-trimmed heads that are firm and heavy for their size with fresh color. Early spring cabbage is not as firm as win-

ter varieties, which are more suitable for storage. Red cabbage and green cabbage are alike except for their color.

Remove outside leaves; wash cabbage. Shred or cut into wedges.

Tip: Cook cabbage quickly in small amount of water. Exposure to air will cause loss of some nutrients; use soon after cooking.

Tip: When cutting cabbage into wedges, leave about ¼ inch of the core; it will hold the leaves together as they cook.

Tip: Add 2 tablespoons lemon juice or vinegar to cooking water to keep red cabbage from turning purple.

Tip: To separate leaves from cabbage head to use for stuffed cabbage rolls, remove core, cover cabbage with boiling water and let stand 10 minutes. Remove leaves that have softened and repeat procedure. If leaves are not pliable enough to roll, continue to soak in boiling water about 5 minutes.

Carrots

Look for firm, nicely shaped orange carrots. Avoid carrots with large green area at top; this indicates sunburn.

Scrape carrots with vegetable parer or knife to save nutrients close to the skin.

Cauliflower

Choose a white or slightly creamy white, firm and compact head; the size of the head has no relation to quality. If small green leaves are attached, they should be crisp and bright green in color, which indicate freshness.

Remove outer leaves and stalk at base; wash cauliflower. Break into small pieces and serve raw in salads. Leave whole or separate into flowerets before cooking.

Tip: Add 1 teaspoon of lemon juice to the cooking water to preserve white color.

Celery (Golden Heart, Pascal)

Whether you buy Golden Heart, which is bleached white, or Pascal, which is green, choose crisp stalks with fresh green leaves. The inside of the stalks should be smooth; puffiness indicates poor celery.

Celery can be braised, whole or sliced, in beef broth until tender.

Tip: Celery leaves are nice for stuffings, soups, salads and garnishes.

Corn

Look for corn with fresh green husks and kernels that are tender, milky and plump. More than 200 varieties of sweet corn offer kernels that are white or yellow or a mixture of both on each cob.

Tip: Cook corn soon after picking or refrigerate it unhusked until ready to use. Remove husk and silk just before cooking.

Tip: For more tender corn, cook in unsalted water with 1 tablespoon sugar and 1 tablespoon lemon juice for each gallon of water.

Cucumbers

Look for small, firm, fresh cucumbers with a deep green color; dull green or yellow color indicates poor quality. European cucumbers (about 2 inches in diameter and 12 to 20 inches in length) should be crisp and lighter green in color than common varieties.

Wash and slice cucumbers or cut lengthwise into sticks (do not pare) for relish trays or garnish for tall drinks. Pare and slice to use in sandwiches, or marinate and serve with sour cream. European cucumbers, which are almost seedless, can be used in the same way.

Greens

Mild-flavored—Beet Top, Chicory (outer leaves), Collards, Dandelion greens, Spinach; Strong-flavored—Kale, Mustard, Swiss Chard, Turnip Top.

Wash greens several times in water, lifting out each time; drain.

Tip: Cook delicate greens a very short time in only the water that clings to the leaves.

Lettuce

Choose iceberg lettuce heads that are firm but not hard, with no sign of rusty-looking tips. Other types of lettuce include butterhead, with soft leaves and a delicate flavor; romaine, with long, dark green leaves and a stronger flavor than iceberg; and leaf, with a crisp texture and mild flavor.

Tip: To remove the core from iceberg lettuce, strike core end against a flat surface, twist and lift out.

Mushrooms

Choose firm mushrooms with smooth, creamy-white to light-brown caps with closed "veil" around base of cap. Mushroom size is no indication of tenderness or quality.

Trim a thin slice from bottoms of stems that appear brown and dry. Rinse mushrooms carefully in cool water; blot with a towel. Do not rinse mushrooms until ready to use. Slice and serve raw in salads; stuff and broil or bake large, whole caps.

Tip: When serving mushrooms alone, cook quickly to retain shape, moisture and texture. Cook longer when mixed with other foods to impart full mushroom flavor.

Tip: Add 1 teaspoon lemon juice to 1 pound mushrooms when panfrying to retain white color and add flavor.

Onions (Dry, Green, Leeks or Shallots)

Choose dry onions (with yellow, white or red skins) that are firm, unblemished and well shaped with dry, papery skins. Green onions, also known as scallions, should have crisp, green tops and 2 to 3 inches of white root. Leeks should have crisp, firm stalks with white bulbs and bright green tops; smaller leeks are more tender and are best served raw. Shallots have bulbs made up of cloves.

Slip the skins from dry onions under running cold water or pour boiling water over them before paring to prevent eyes from watering. Wash and trim green onions to remove roots and loose layers of skin. Leave about 3 inches of green top for flavor and color. Trim leeks by removing root, dry outer skin and blemished leaves. Wash leeks several times in water; drain. Slice and serve raw in salads or marinate for appetizers. Bake, broil or cook in liquid and use in stews, soups and sauces.

Tip: After eating onions, eat several sprigs of parsley that have been dipped in salt or vinegar to sweeten breath.

Tip: To keep onions whole and prevent inner section from slipping out while boiling, cut an "X" about ¼ inch deep in the stem end before cooking.

Peas, Green

Look for bright green, fairly large pea pods that are well-filled and tender.

Tip: For sweet, tender peas, wash, shell and quickly cook soon after picking.

Peppers (Mild-flavored—Green and Red Bell; Hot-flavored—Chili and Cayenne)

Choose well-shaped, thick-walled and firm peppers with uniform color. Fresh bell peppers are mild and sweet fleshed. Hot peppers are often dried and sold in strings.

Wash peppers; remove stems and seeds by cutting into two sections from base almost to stem. Pull sections apart; stem end with most of the seeds will pop out. Cut sections into strips or dice. Remove stems, seeds and membranes to use whole; stuff and bake or slice into rings.

Tip: Remember, the larger the pepper, the milder its flavor; the smaller the pepper, the hotter to taste.

Potatoes (Round Red, Round White, Russet, Long White)

Look for fairly clean, smooth, firm and well-shaped potatoes to avoid waste in paring. Uniform size will ensure even cooking.

Wash potatoes or gently scrub with vegetable brush. Leave skins on whenever possible or pare thinly with a vegetable parer; remove eyes before cooking.

Tip: To retain white color of pared potatoes before cooking, toss them with ascorbic acid mixture or a small amount of lemon juice.

Tip: Avoid soaking potatoes in cold water for a long period, which causes vitamin loss.

Tip: Boiling potatoes in their skins, which can be eaten or slipped off easily after cooking, saves nutrients.

Spinach (See Greens, page 106)

Squash (Soft-shelled and Hard-shelled)

Choose soft-shelled squash (often called summer squash, although available all win-

ter), which is firm and well-shaped with shiny, smooth skin. Choose hard-shelled squash (often called winter squash, although also available in late summer and fall), which is heavy with a hard, dark green or yellow-orange rind.

Wash soft-shelled squash and remove stem and blossom ends, but do not pare. Cut into ½-inch slices or cubes to boil, broil, panfry or bake. Cut hard-shelled squash in serving pieces with a chef knife; remove seeds and fibers with a serrated grapefruit spoon or tablespoon before baking or microwaving.

Tip: Spaghetti squash can be baked or microwaved whole if the shell is first pierced to allow steam to escape while cooking. To serve cooked spaghetti squash, cut squash into halves crosswise; scoop out seeds. Unwind spaghetti-like flesh with fork and serve as you would pasta.

Tomatoes

Choose firm, well-shaped, fully ripe tomatoes that are heavy in relation to their size.

Tip: To peel, dip tomato into boiling water 30 seconds, then into cold water. Or scrape surface of tomato with dull side of knife to loosen; peel with sharp side of knife.

Speed up ripening of a slightly green tomato by placing in a brown paper bag; as the tomato ripens, it gives off a natural gas, ethylene, which hastens the ripening process when confined in a closed area.

INDEX

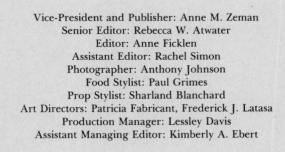

Vice-President and Publisher: Anne M. Zeman
Senior Editor: Rebecca W. Atwater
Editor: Anne Ficklen
Assistant Editor: Rachel Simon
Photographer: Anthony Johnson
Food Stylist: Paul Grimes
Prop Stylist: Sharland Blanchard
Art Directors: Patricia Fabricant, Frederick J. Latasa
Production Manager: Lessley Davis
Assistant Managing Editor: Kimberly A. Ebert